LEATHERNECK WARRIOR

LEATHERNECK WARRIOR

General Lemuel C. Shepherd Jr.

Colonel Richard D. Camp USMC (Ret.)

CASEMATE
Pennsylvania & Yorkshire

Published in the United States of America and Great Britain in 2025 by
CASEMATE PUBLISHERS
1950 Lawrence Road, Havertown, PA 19083, USA
and
47 Church Street, Barnsley, S70 2AS, UK

Copyright © 2025 Colonel Richard D. Camp USMC (Ret.)

Hardcover Edition: ISBN 978-1-63624-506-5
Digital Edition: ISBN 978-1-63624-507-2

A CIP record for this book is available from the British Library

All rights reserved. No part of this book may be reproduced or transmitted in any form or by any means, electronic or mechanical including photocopying, recording or by any information storage and retrieval system, without permission from the publisher in writing.

Printed and bound in the United Kingdom by CPI Group (UK) Ltd, Croydon, CR0 4YY
Typeset in India by DiTech Publishing Services

For a complete list of Casemate titles, please contact:

CASEMATE PUBLISHERS (US)
Telephone (610) 853-9131
Fax (610) 853-9146
Email: casemate@casematepublishers.com
www.casematepublishers.com

CASEMATE PUBLISHERS (UK)
Telephone (0)1226 734350
Email: casemate@casemateuk.com
www.casemateuk.com

Cover image: General Lemuel C. Shepherd Jr., commandant of the USMC. (Virginia Military Institute)

The Publisher's authorised representative in the EU for product safety is Authorised Rep Compliance Ltd., Ground Floor, 71 Lower Baggot Street, Dublin D02 P593, Ireland.
www.arccompliance.com

For Jim Mattis, No Better Friend.

Contents

Prelude ix

1	Molding the Man, February 1896–April 1917	1
2	Developing the Warrior, September 1916–May 1917	9
3	First to Fight, June 1917	15
4	*Je Suis Américain*, July–September 1917	19
5	The Blooding, March–May 1918	29
6	Bois de la Brigade de Marine (Belleau Wood), May 31–June 5, 1918	37
7	Wounded in Action, June 1918	43
8	Saint-Mihiel All-American Offensive, September 10–16, 1918	49
9	Blanc Mont (White Mountain), October 1–9, 1918	53
10	Streets of New York, August 1919	59
11	Mapping Belleau Wood, September 1919–December 1920	63
12	Interwar Years, 1920–1943	67
13	Striking Ninth, 1943–1944	73
14	The Green Inferno, January 1944	77
15	1st Marine Brigade, Operation *Stevedore*, July–August 1944	83
16	6th Marine Division, Operation *Iceberg*, 1 April–21 June 1945	91
17	North China, September–December 1945	115
18	Assistant Commandant, March 1946–April 1948	123
19	Battle of the Potomac, May 1948	127

20	Fleet Marine Force, Pacific, June 1950	133
21	The Great Gamble, September 15, 1950	143
22	Attack of General Winter, November 1950	157
23	20th Commandant of the Marine Corps, January 1952–January 1956	163
24	Retirement, January 1, 1956	169

Appendix A: Military Background	173
Appendix B: Military Decorations	175
Endnotes	177
Bibliography	187
Index	189

Prelude

In 1984, as the director of the 12th Marine Corps District, I hosted a quarterly recruiting conference at the San Diego Marine Corps Recruit Depot Officers' Club for my recruiting station commanding officers. I invited General Lemuel C. Shepherd Jr., former commandant of the Marine Corps, to attend and share his experiences in the Corps with us.

A staff car picked up the 84-year-old general at his home in La Jolla, California. Upon his arrival, I escorted him into the officers' club. The general walked with a cane and was noticeably unsteady on his feet. As he struggled up the steps of the club, I overheard a young officer whisper callously, "Who the hell is that old man?" Once he got settled, Shepherd, who was nearly blind, invited the officers to introduce themselves. As one introduced himself, Shepherd stopped him and asked in his soft tidewater accent if he was any relation to a Marine officer he knew. "Yes, sir," the officer replied, "he was my father." Shepherd then went into a long account of searching for the remains of his father, who had been shot down on a mission over Japan during

General Lemuel C. Shepherd Jr., commandant of the USMC. (Virginia Military Institute)

World War II. Within minutes he totally captivated the officers with his articulate account of recovering the remains, as well as his grasp of military subjects.

Shepherd shared other experiences with us. He talked of serving under General Roy S. Geiger, the only Marine to ever command an American field army, the Tenth Army on Okinawa in 1945. Shepherd commanded the 6th Marine Division during the hellish campaign. He spoke of Geiger's penchant for visiting the front lines. Shepherd related a humorous story of one such visit: Geiger nonchalantly walked up on a squad of Marines lying prone on the ground behind cover in a furious firefight with the Japanese on the next ridge. Almost immediately one Marine shouted, "Get down, you old fool! Do you want to get us all killed!" Geiger sheepishly replied, "Sorry son," turned, and sauntered away.

Toward the end of the conversation, one of my officers asked, "General, what was the worst thing you faced in your 42 years of service?" Shepherd did not miss a beat: "Machine guns at Belleau Wood," he answered, referring to the famous World War I battle in France. There was stunned silence. The officers stared at the old man with a new respect. Shepherd was the living embodiment of a Marine Corps legend, for the battle of Belleau Wood was synonymous with Marine valor and sacrifice.

CHAPTER I

Molding the Man, February 1896–April 1917

Lemuel Cornick "Lem" Shepherd Jr. was born into a tidewater family on a cold, snowy night on February 10, 1896, in the three-story brick home of his parents in Norfolk, Virginia. Known as "Lem" by his schoolmates, he was a ninth-generation American; his family traced its roots back to 1652, when an ancestor, Thomas Shepherd, emigrated from England to become a prosperous tobacco farmer. Lem's father, a well-known Norfolk physician, had one of the largest obstetrical practices in Virginia. His mother, Emma Cartwright Shepherd, was a teacher at Leach Wood Seminary, a private girls' school in the city. During the Civil War, the Shepherds supported the Confederacy: Lem's grandfather, John Camp Shepherd, served in the 15th Virginia Cavalry and was wounded during the siege of Petersburg. After the war, he returned to the land and opened a small general store on his property. The store was successful, producing enough income to send his son to medical school. His father's uncle, Lemuel Cornick, was killed in a cavalry skirmish at Chancellorsville.[1]

Shepherd enjoyed a comfortable, happy childhood. The Shepherds' neighborhood was filled with children of Lem's age, with whom he enjoyed a friendship that endured over the years. He enjoyed the neighborhood pickup games of baseball. His father owned two horses; Lem rode them frequently and developed a love for horses. His family was comfortable enough financially to send Lem to St. George's, a private school, and later to Norfolk Academy and Maury High School, where he played football and managed the high school's track team. He walked to school with his friends, often stopping at a little doughnut and coffee stand on the way. It was run by a Jamaican nicknamed Cheap Charlie who spoke with a very pronounced British accent that the youngsters loved to listen to. By age 14, Lem had grown into a slender youngster of medium build with a warm and outgoing disposition that brought him many friends.[2]

VMI Cadet Shepherd

Several of Lem's friends and high school classmates attended the Virginia Military Institute and convinced him to apply. In the fall of 1913, at age 16, he entered VMI as a fourth class cadet or "rat," as the incoming cadets were called. He hadn't planned on a military career. His parents wanted him to follow in his father's footsteps and become a doctor. Initially he studied electrical engineering—he was a ham operator, one of the first around Norfolk—but later switched to civil engineering because he liked fieldwork. He had a cousin working in Nicaragua as a civil engineer, and civil engineering sounded more exciting. Lem thought the decision to attend VMI was the most fortunate he ever made and one that he never regretted.[3]

Life at VMI in those days was a rugged existence. The cadets entered the fall semester in early September and did not return home until the later part of June. There were no Christmas furloughs and only five one-day holidays throughout the year—Founders Day, November 10; Thanksgiving; Christmas; New Year's; and New Market Day, May 15 (on May 15, 1864, the

Lemuel C. Shepherd Jr. as a cadet, 1916. (Virginia Military Institute)

Corps of Cadets fought as a unit at the battle of New Market, in which 10 cadets "died on the field of honor")—when they could relax in the barracks. "Reveille" went at 6:15 a.m., breakfast was at 7:00 a.m., and classes began at 8:00 a.m. and lasted until 4:00 p.m., when the Corps of Cadets fell out for an hour of drill, followed by the Sunset Parade. Call to Quarters and study hour followed supper with "Taps" at 10:00 p.m. The life of a fourth classman was an unpleasant existence as hazing prevailed and a "rat" was always subject to the whim of upperclassmen.[4]

Three cadets were assigned to a room, except the tower rooms, which were occupied by four first classmen. The barrack rooms were about 20 feet square and were equipped with three folding wooden cots and mattresses that were called "hays." A square table stood in the center of the room and a metal washstand in the corner. There was a tin dipper and a water bucket that had to be filled from a spigot on the stoop. A stand of wooden shelves was provided. Clothing and uniforms were hung against the wall. Cots and mattresses were required to be folded and stacked against the wall during the day.[5]

On the side of the room opposite the doorway there were two large windows that, together with the door, were required to be kept open from "Taps" to "Reveille." There was one small radiator to a room. It was thought that the rugged life at VMI, with its strict discipline, physical drills, and regimented existence, did much to develop the qualities of manhood and build character among the young gentlemen.

Shepherd was an average student and upon graduation stood in the middle of his class. In his second year, he failed one of the major subjects and had to attend summer school to make up the credit. At the end of his "rat" year, he was appointed to the rank of cadet corporal but then lost the stripes when he was caught firing skyrockets from his barracks window on New Year's Eve—an act that he always regretted. In his second year, he joined the Tiqua Club, one of the three social societies that were organized at VMI, a membership that he prized for the remainder of his life. He participated in football and track but never lettered. Socially, he looked forward to the formal five-times-a-year coed dances.[6]

In February 1917 it became apparent, during his first class year, that the United States might become involved in World War I. In January,

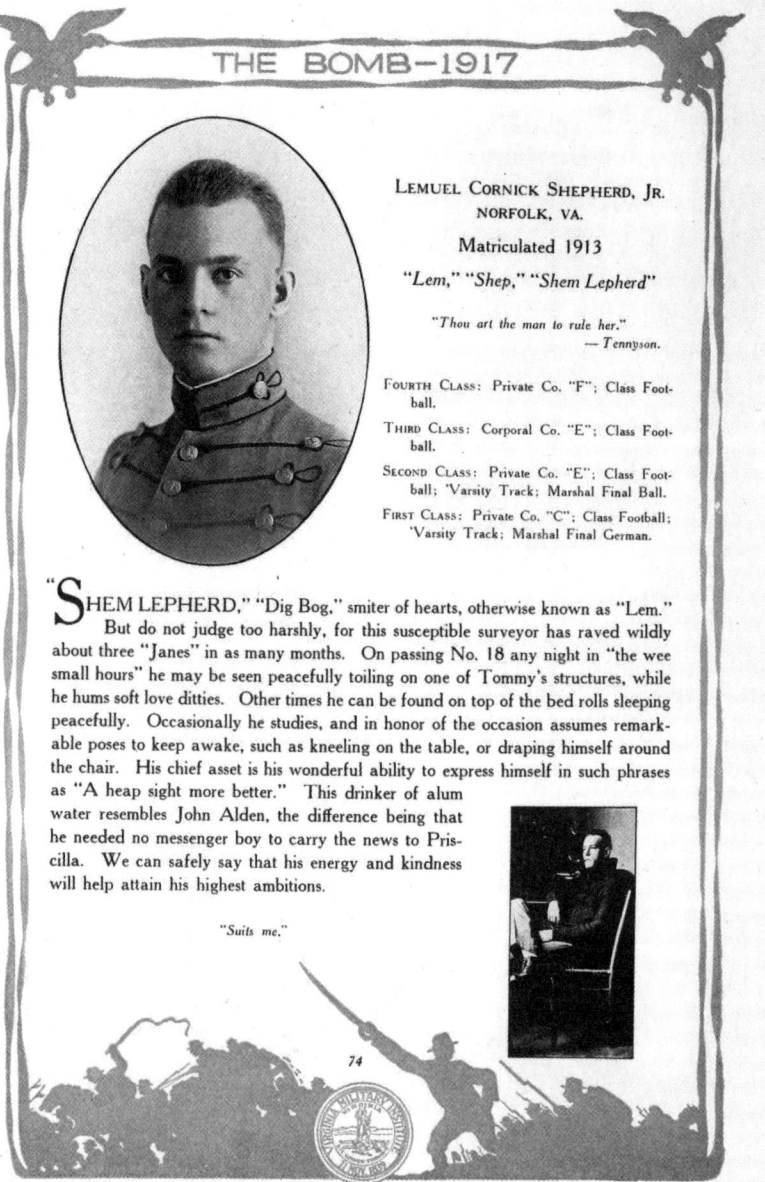

Page taken from VMI's yearbook, *The Bomb*. (Virginia Military Institute)

Britain deciphered the Zimmermann telegram, which offered United States territory to Mexico in return for joining the German cause. A month later Germany resumed unrestricted submarine warfare, which resulted in the United States severing diplomatic ties with Germany. And finally, on April 6, Congress declared war: "that a state of war exists between the United States and the Imperial German Government …"

With the declaration of war, Shepherd followed the example of several classmates and applied to the commandant, Colonel Harry Hodges, for an Army commission. Hodges was sympathetic but told Shepherd that while he'd like to recommend him, there were no commissions available. Disappointed, Shepherd asked him about a Marine Corps commission. A year earlier, the Major General Commandant George Barnett had given the commencement address in full-dress uniform, which had made a lasting impression on the young cadet. He had seen Marine officers in Norfolk, but he had never seen them in dress uniforms. He was also keen on the idea of serving aboard ship rather than being in the trenches with the Army. Unfortunately, the 10 Marine reserve commissions were also gone, but Hodges held out some hope that the services' rapid wartime expansion might generate additional openings.[7]

On May 18, 1917, Congress enacted the Selective Service Act conscripting men into the armed forces. Three months later, the size of the Marine Corps doubled under the Naval Appropriations Act from its 1913 level of 340 officers and 10,000 men to 600 officers and 15,000 men. Shepherd's opportunity arrived. He typed an application requesting a Marine appointment, marched over to the superintendent's office, and presented it to General Edward W. "Old Nick" Nichols. Nichols agreed to telegraph the commandant of the Marine Corps and recommend that the application be given favorable consideration.[8]

Within days, 21-year-old Shepherd received orders to appear before an examining board at the Marine Barracks, 8th and I Streets, in Washington. He had to borrow money for a ticket on the midnight train from Lynchburg to Washington. The train was so crowded that he had to stand up for the entire six-hour trip. When he arrived in Washington the next morning, he rented a room, washed up, shaved, and reported for the nine o'clock examination. He reported to Colonel Charles A. Doyen, commanding officer of the barracks and president of the examining board. Doyen turned him over to Captain Paul T. "Bobo" Dessez, USN, a rough, gruff old seagoing bull surgeon, the senior member of the medical examining board. Shepherd, at a lean 120 pounds, was concerned about passing the physical because he was underweight. Dessez took his blood pressure, looked him over, and asked if he had ever had a case of the clap or the piles. Coming from a proper Virginia family, Shepherd replied rather indignantly that he had not. After completing the perfunctory exam, Dessez pronounced Shepherd fit for service. Following the physical examination, he returned to the examining board for a personal interview. It only lasted a few minutes as apparently the recommendation General Nichols had given him was sufficient to meet the academic requirements for a commission.[9]

Shepherd reported back to Colonel Doyen, who told him that he could be sworn in immediately as a Marine reserve second lieutenant or wait several months to receive a regular commission. Shepherd raised his hand and was sworn in on April 15, 1917, just 10 days after war had been declared.

Even though he was a newly commissioned Marine officer, he still ranked as a cadet at VMI. This imbalance lasted only a few days when, in the third week of April, Superintendent Nichols received a telegram from the Marine Corps requesting him to graduate the new officers as soon as possible. The annual report of VMI noted:

> Upon the recommendation of the Academic Board and by the authority of the Advisory Committee of the Board of Visitors, thirty members of the first class were graduated May 2nd. These young men, needed by their government and on its request, were sent to training camps established for officers. Many of them will enter the regular service ... as Second Lieutenants of the army and of the Marine Corps.

Shepherd and his colleagues were simultaneously graduated from VMI on May 3 and called to active duty. Shepherd always remembered the date because it was the day Stonewall Jackson, a great hero at VMI, won the battle of Chancellorsville. Before the battle, Jackson was quoted as saying, "VMI will be heard from today." Shepherd followed that motto throughout his life.[10]

Two weeks later, Shepherd and Cadet Charlie Nash boarded the Atlantic Coast Line train for Parris Island, South Carolina, an insect-infested spit of swampland near Beaufort. "PI," as it was called by generations of Marines, was an isolated outpost that could only be reached by boat. At six o'clock the next morning the two got off the pullman at Yamasee Junction, the depot's initial receiving point, and boarded the Charleston & Western Carolina Railway, which took them to Port Royal. Here a motorsailor awaited them and an hour later docked at Parris Island. Shepherd never forgot the experience. As he was disembarking close by the old dry dock, he was greeted by several of his schoolmates who had graduated the previous year (1916) who were on their way for duty in Haiti and San Domingo. Shepherd thought how lucky they were to be on their way to a foreign country. As it turned out, Shepherd was the fortunate one, as most of this group spent the next two years in the jungles fighting bandits in Haiti and never got to France.[11]

Shepherd and Nash reported to the Officers School of Application, which had been established in a tent camp for newly commissioned officers. On the first day of training, they were rudely awakened by a bugler blowing "Reveille" inside their tent, a prank courtesy of fellow students who had reported in prior to their arrival. The two were issued a number of professional books; among the most important were *The Landing-Force Manual*, *The Marine Corps Manual*, *Navy Regulations*, and several other service publications. Instruction covered infantry drill regulations, bayonet training, bombing (hand grenades), small unit tactics, military engineering, administration, military law, and poison gas. In two weeks at the rifle range, they were taught the nomenclature of the rifle and pistol and the correct positions for aiming and firing. Shepherd spent countless hours "snapping in" to condition his muscles and perfect the correct firing positions. At the end of qualification week, Shepherd qualified as a sharpshooter, missing expert by only a few points.

Just two weeks after reporting, Shepherd's class of officers were ordered to report to the commanding officer, who asked them if they would volunteer for duty with the 5th Marine Regiment that was headed overseas. Shepherd and two friends immediately held up their hands, even though they were in the dark as to what their assignments would be.

At the time, all they wanted was to join a combat unit and begin duties as Marine officers. Within 48 hours, the three received orders to join the 5th Regiment of Marines that was forming at the Philadelphia Navy Yard. Since Shepherd had four days proceed time before reporting, he decided to stop over for a day in Norfolk to see his parents and his grandmother, a grand old Southern lady and unreconstructed Confederate. He wore his khaki uniform. His grandmother admitted being pleased to see him in khaki rather than his blue uniform because she never wanted to see her grandson wearing a Yankee blue uniform.[12]

CHAPTER 2

Developing the Warrior, September 1916–May 1917

Shepherd arrived at the Philadelphia Navy Yard on June 5 and was given command of the 4th Platoon, 55th Company, a big wartime unit of about 250 men—half veterans, half recruits. The 2nd Battalion, 5th Regiment of Marines was commanded by the eccentric Major Frederic May "Fritz" Wise, the nemesis of junior officers. Behind his back, they called him "Dopey" or sometimes "Fritz" because of his authoritarian, Prussian-style leadership. Shepherd told the author that Wise prefaced every order to him with, "Goddam you Shepherd." Wise was an old-time Marine. He entered the Corps before the turn of the century and saw his first action during the Boxer Rebellion, when the Marines were sent to China to protect American citizens from the wrath of the Society of Righteous and Harmonious Fists, popularly known as "Boxers." Fritz, then stationed at the Cavite Naval Base, was a member of the ship's landing party aboard the armored cruiser USS *Brooklyn* that landed at Tientsin to maintain order. At one point Wise was ordered to take a detachment to protect the salt commissioner's yamen, which held a "vast" treasure of "sycee" (silver). In the process of "protecting" the treasure—a pile of the precious metal 30 feet long, 30 feet wide, and four feet high—Wise "helped himself" to the tune of $5,000 worth of the silver, a handsome sum in those days. A civilian friend arranged to "launder" it for him. In Wise's defense, if there was one, several other Marines participated in the "help yourself" scheme.[1]

Wise was proud of his ties with the old Marine Corps. In his view, the "old-timers" were the backbone of the Corps and there were damned few of them left. He lived by the credo of work hard, drink hard, and fight hard. He was unrepentant and knew there were many who "questioned his ancestry," but he offered no excuses for his toughness. He was readying the battalion for war, and he would accept nothing less than perfection. One story about his callousness that circulated among the junior officers involved a troublesome Marine who passed away. At his funeral, Wise is reported to have ordered the band to play the 1897 ballad "He Was Always in the Way." Wise claimed that he had entered the Corps under martinets who accepted no excuses and required results and that this left its mark on him. It can be said that Wise picked up his "difficult" personality from those he encountered as a young officer. Shepherd told the author that Wise always ended any order to him with, "Goddam you, Mr. Shepherd!" Fritz Wise was described as a combination of ability and hardheadedness, as an even-tempered man who was mad all the time.[2]

The regiment was billeted in tents at the Navy Yard and was in the throes of reorganization from peace to war strength. It consisted of three infantry battalions (1st, 2nd, and 3rd) and a machine gun battalion. The 2nd Battalion consisted of five companies: the 18th (from January 16, 1918, on, under Captain L. S. Wass), 43rd (Captain Joseph D. Murray), 51st (Captain Lloyd W. Williams), 55th (Captain Henry M. Butler), and the 23rd Machine Gun Company (Captain George H. Osterhout Jr.). For the first six months in France, the regiment was attached to the First Army Division.[3]

Shepherd immediately began the process of absorbing the recruits who had swarmed into the recruiting stations under the banner of "First to Fight." Shepherd was in command of one platoon in the 55th Company, under Captain Butler. In those days a Marine infantry company was organized with eight men in a squad, six squads to a platoon (and several file closers and guides bringing platoon strength to 52 men), four platoons per company, along with a company headquarters section. Shepherd recalled that he stayed up all the first night issuing uniforms to men joining the company. Confusion reigned as new recruits just finishing training and several hundred veterans who had been recalled from duty in Haiti and San Domingo came pouring in. The 55th Company was brought up to strength from fewer than 100 men to 250 men in a period of a

Marines "crapped out" in front of the Navy Yard barracks. Note the stacked rifles in the background and the "salty" campaign covers worn by the men. (Marine Corps Archives)

few days. Wise closely scrutinized them and told his officers that he didn't want the sick, the lame, or the lazy, or any man who had the slightest thing wrong, including the older noncommissioned officers. One old veteran personally begged Wise to be added to the sailing roster. Wise knew him, and, although the man was 47 years old, Wise relented and added his name to the roster. Wise admitted that it was one of the best decisions he made. Those veterans who survived the close screening were worth it, as they taught the recruits basic military subjects and instilled in them the ethos of the Corps.[4]

Less than a week after reporting for duty, Shepherd received word that the battalion was going to ship out, but no one knew where they were going. Everything was in confusion. The transport USS *Hancock*, a small naval transport, arrived on the night of June 1 and immediately began embarking troops and equipment. Conditions aboard the ship were extremely uncomfortable; the men were packed in like sardines. The docks were a frenzy of activity as frantic quartermasters struggled to meet the sailing deadline. Finally, at dusk on June 11, the *Hancock* slipped quietly away from the dock. Just a few officers' wives were present as a band played "Auld Lang Syne." Late the next day the ship entered the outer harbor of New York and dropped anchor for several days, awaiting orders, exemplifying the old military adage, "Hurry up and wait." To add insult to injury, the *Hancock* was too slow and could not sail with the first convoy of fast ships.[5]

The newly commissioned USS *Henderson*, named for the fifth commandant, General Archibald Henderson, and built expressly as a troop transport for the Marine Corps, was substituted. The transport arrived in New York on June 12 from a trial run and immediately reembarked the Marines off the *Hancock*. Shepherd led his heavily laden men up the *Henderson*'s gangway and followed guides to their berthing compartments. Encumbered with rifles and heavy marching order they struggled to negotiate the narrow, twisting passageways. Equipment caught on bulkhead projections; men tripped on projections in the unfamiliar deck. Tempers grew short. For the unwary, hatch coamings (openings between sections of the ship) offered their own brand of torture. The new men who did not duck collided with the vertical steel boundary around the hatches and found themselves flat on their backs, nursing sore heads and bruised egos. The physical exertion, combined with the heat below decks, caused them to sweat, soaking their uniforms and causing even more discomfort. Somehow or other the troops embarked, and supplies were loaded and stored in the holds. Shepherd recalled heaving a sigh of relief after getting his platoon safely aboard.

The newly embarked Marines were faced not only with a new environment but also with an entirely new jargon: *deck* (floor), *overhead* (ceiling), *ladder* (stairway), *passageway* (hallway), *head* (toilet), *galley* (kitchen). They learned other Navy traditions, the origins of which they neither knew nor cared about. The youngsters became the brunt of harmless time-honored pranks, played on them by old sea dogs. Even so,

USS *Henderson* AP-1. (Naval History and Heritage Command)

the very newness of the adventure—going off to war—made it exciting and somewhat strangely romantic.

Shepherd soon found out that he would not be joining his friends in the tropics; he was headed for the battlefields of France.

Transportation Has Been Arranged

The fact that the Marines were going to France at all was solely due to the unremitting effort of Major General Commandant George Barnett, who launched a personal campaign to convince Secretary of War Newton D. Baker to use Marines. Barnett recalled the slogan "First to Fight" on the recruiting posters, and he didn't want that slogan made to look ridiculous. Despite a shortage of trained men, the Army did not want Marines and dredged up phony roadblocks, which in the cold light of day proved to be groundless.⁶

Barnett, a socially prominent Washington insider and friend of the president, enlisted his aid. Woodrow Wilson ordered the secretary of war, "in pursuance of the authority vested in [him] by law," to "issue the necessary orders detaching for service with the army a force of Marines to be known as the 5th Regiment of Marines." The secretary penned a note to Barnett with one last ploy, saying, "I'm sorry to have to tell you that it will be utterly impossible for the War Department to furnish transportation for a Marine regiment with the first sailing." Needless to say, General Barnett had an ace up his sleeve. A friend, Admiral W. S. Benson, chief of naval operations, had "reserved" three Navy transports for the Marines. Barnett wrote to Secretary Baker rather tongue in cheek, noting that he should not bother himself further as transportation for the Marines had been arranged. Years later, Shepherd acknowledged the commandant's role. He thought General Barnett deserved a great deal of credit for getting the Marines to France, because the Army fought their deployment tooth and nail.⁷

World War I recruiting poster. Major Albert S. McLemore, head of the corps recruiting efforts during World War I, suggested the slogan, which he drew from the corps hymn. (U.S. Government)

CHAPTER 3

First to Fight, June 1917

"Over the Seas, Let's Go Men"

SONG OF THE MARINES

On June 14, 1917, under cover of darkness, the *Henderson* upped anchor and got underway in the second convoy to sail for France. The convoy had barely left port when it was discovered that the *Henderson* was a long way from being ready for an Atlantic crossing. Nothing seemed to work. Drinking fountains wouldn't function; the green crew didn't know how to operate the oil-burning ranges in the galley; and, more importantly, the ship had neither the gaskets necessary to keep the hatches watertight nor enough lifeboats for the number of embarked troops. A torpedo strike could have wreaked havoc.[1]

It was an exciting adventure for all hands as the convoy sailed eastward surrounded by an anti-submarine screen of destroyers and cruisers. Time passed slowly as the ships steamed slowly toward the combat zone. The young officers had time on their hands and gathered together to share thoughts. Shepherd recalled several discussions among his friends on life expectancy among second lieutenants in combat on the western front. They had been told that it was a matter of days, but as is the case with most young men, they shrugged it off; death was something that happened to others. In a letter home dated January 21, 1918, Shepherd assured his mother that he had decided "a long time ago" that he would return home when the war was over and that he never thought about "going west," the British expression for being killed in action.

Shepherd spent the first few days organizing his platoon, checking equipment, and assigning men to lookout stations and gun crews. He took his turn as the officer of the day, which required constant inspections during the night to ensure that no exposed lights were showing. He also supervised the messing facilities and, despite the crowded conditions, he conducted physical exercise and close-order drill on deck.

The weather was good, but even so, many of the newly embarked Marines were victims of mal de mer. The sight of so many landlubbers hanging over the rail gave the old salts an excuse to taunt the "dying" men with visions of pork fat, bacon, and other mouthwatering delicacies. Despite misgivings about surviving, most of the men recovered within a day or two. Shepherd was not affected and continued to carry out his duties.[2]

The ship conducted daily troop musters and fire and abandon ship drills because of the submarine threat. Between April 1917 and November 1918, four German U-boats sank 10 ships, including two U.S. Navy vessels off the North Carolina coast. Every man was ordered to have his life jacket on his person at all times. The submarine menace was real.

The arrival of the 5th Marines at Saint-Nazaire. (Naval Historical Center)

To emphasize the danger, an escorting destroyer dropped several depth charges close to the convoy. "It was a very tense time," Shepherd noted.[3]

A hundred miles off the coast of France, two German U-boats were spotted, but they didn't attack. The next day, June 27, 1917, the *Henderson* docked at Saint-Nazaire. Shepherd began an intensive seven-month period of training. He looked back on his short time in the Corps. "I graduated from VMI on the third of May, reported to Parris Island for duty on the nineteenth, and landed in France with a platoon of Marines on the twenty-seventh of June—all within a period of two months. That's moving!"[4]

CHAPTER 4

Je Suis Américain, July–September 1917

Gondrecourt Training Area, July to September 1917

On the following morning, Wise ordered Shepherd to go ashore with a detail of enlisted personnel and set up a tent camp for the battalion. Shepherd protested that he had never laid out a tent camp, but Wise wasn't having any. "Shepherd," he shouted, "Goddamn you, go lay out a camp. I didn't ask you anything; I told you something. Now, Goddamn it, go lay out a camp." Shepherd rounded up several veteran NCOs and proceeded to the site. When they arrived, they found all the tent canvas dumped on the ground. After laying out the camp, they were able to erect enough tents to satisfy Wise. Shepherd said afterward that even though he had never done anything like it before, the camp setup showed what you can do when you have to.[1]

Within a few days, the battalion received orders to embark by train for a two-day trip to the small village of Menacourt in the Gondrecourt training area, some 15 or 20 miles south of Verdun. The men were crowded into small boxcars labeled *40 Hommes et 8 Chevaux* (40 men and 8 horses). The officers occupied a so-called first-class coach in the rear of the train. The train was unlike anything the men had ever seen before. The flimsy boxcars were about 14 feet long and equipped with a diabolical arrangement of heavy plank seats along the sides that were convenient during the day but made it absolutely impossible to get any sleep at night.[2]

It took 48 hours for the train to cross France as there were frequent stops to change engines. Rations consisting mostly of soup, coffee, and a chunk of bread were issued en route from field kitchens set up at various stations. The coffee was laced with cognac, and once the men discovered this, they took every opportunity to fill their canteens, which caused some concern among the officers. Whenever the train stopped at a railroad station or one of the larger towns, crowds of French civilians gathered on the platform and gave the Marines an enthusiastic welcome, often presenting bouquets of flowers or bottles of red wine.

Arriving at Menacourt, Shepherd was surprised by the band of the 115th Chasseurs Alpins playing "The Star-Spangled Banner" and a raft of children crying, "*Soyez les bienvenus*" (welcome). The French military quickly assigned the battalion billets. The men were quartered in stables

Arrival of the 1st and 2nd Battalions, 5th Marines at the Gondrecourt training area. (The Doughboy Foundation)

and hay lofts, the officers in homes of the locals. French law stated that the owner of each house was required to provide any unoccupied rooms for billeting Army personnel quartered in the area. On the front of every French home in the combat zone there was stenciled in black lettering the number of rooms available for billeting. The local mayor also maintained a list of billets in this town that he provided the military billeting officer.[3]

Shepherd's billet was in a one-story, stucco-covered, three-room house. The elderly owner did her cooking over an open fire in the street-level room. The room behind the kitchen was her bedroom. Shepherd occupied the third room, which had a window facing a small barnyard, where the animals were kept. It was necessary to pass through the old lady's bedroom to get to his room, but this did not seem to bother her in the least. In the evenings, the old woman was generally sitting by the fire cooking her dinner. Occasionally Shepherd joined her and would ask her to pronounce the words and phrases in his pocket French dictionary.

Fortunately, Shepherd had studied French at VMI and could at least carry on a conversation if the person spoke slowly. It was surprising, however, how much more French he picked up as his ear became attuned to the language. Although he never learned to speak French grammatically, he was able to understand the language and carry on a normal conversation about mundane subjects.

Outside the front door of his billet, as was the case in other houses in the village, there was a large manure pile in which he was told the French placed their Camembert cheeses for maturing. In those days a peasant's existence in the small villages throughout France was a simple one with few luxuries.

Blue Devils

A day after arriving at Menacourt, the battalion began training with the highly respected 115th Battalion Chasseurs Alpins, the "Blue Devils," an elite corps of veteran mountain troops. They earned their nickname because of their dark blue uniforms, including blue berets, and superior fighting qualities. Shepherd acknowledged that the Chasseurs were a

115th Battalion Alpine Chasseurs instructing U.S. Marines. (NARA)

proven corps of elite troops, but he was disbelieving of their boast of being the best fighters, the best drinkers, and the best lovers in France. Shepherd learned that that last characteristic was uppermost in the minds of all Frenchmen.[4]

The 115th Battalion was commanded by a tall, blond major from Normandy by the name of Toussaint. Shepherd remembered him as a big man with a clipped mustache and reddish hair. On occasion, when he was speaking forcefully, his rounded, pink cheeks looked like two ripe apples. His chest was covered by several rows of ribbons, which included the highest French decorations and a number of campaign medals for service in North Africa and other colonial possessions. He was definitely a French professional soldier of the finest type and obviously a leader.[5]

The battalion spent the entire summer training with the Blue Devils, who paired one of their companies with its Marine counterpart. It was a novel experience since there were only a few interpreters and most of the training consisted in following the movements of the French. Initially, the Marines were directed to use French commands, including close order, but this caused problems and did not last for long. VMI had given Shepherd a smattering of the language, which stood him in good stead in understanding the commands and translating them to English.

"Fritz" Wise related that every morning right after breakfast the battalion marched out to the training area, where they met the Blue Devil instructors and commenced digging a series of trenches for a battalion sector on a plateau near Menacourt. The war in France had become a stalemate, with each side entrenched in a series of trenches that stretched from the North Sea coast of Belgium southward through France to the Swiss border. A battalion sector included a frontline trench, protected by tangled lines of barbed wire; a support trench several hundred yards behind the frontline trench; and a reserve line several hundred yards behind that. Shepherd was taught to construct the trench in a zigzag manner to prevent enfilade or sweeping fire. He also led his platoon in practice trench raids and instructed in the positioning of weapons—machine guns, mortars, hand and rifle grenades—for trench line defense. Instruction was also given in the "field stripping" of all infantry arms and in the firing of hand and rifle grenades and the submachine gun. There were also a number of attack exercises with the artillery firing live ammunition.

In January, newly promoted First Lieutenant Shepherd attended a French school for platoon officers (*Chefs de Section*), run by the U.S. Army's I Corps at Gondrecourt, whose emphasis was on infantry tactics and weapons. Shepherd recalled the chief instructor, a British NCO, continually shouting a single refrain: "Blood on the bayonet, boys, blood on the bayonet." The school was a welcome break from the battalion's hectic training schedule and one that Shepherd enjoyed. He claimed it was the best duty he had. Early in the morning the attendees were trucked to a

Marines reinforce a training trench at Marine Corps Base Quantico, circa 1918. (USMC)

Sandbags between trenches, Quantico, Virginia, 1917. (USMC)

small village about 30 miles away from Menacourt. Classes started at eight o'clock and ended at 11 o'clock for a five-course lunch, including wine and champagne, in the French officers' mess. After lunch the French officers would sing their various battle songs, which the Americans soon learned to join in. They would then retire to the local churchyard and take a siesta among its ancient gravestones. At two o'clock the students assembled for the afternoon class, which lasted until four o'clock, when they returned to Menacourt. Shepherd learned a great deal about French tactics and combat operations at the school.[6]

In a January 1918 letter to his mother, Shepherd wrote:

> I Corps Schools
> Gondrecourt, France
> January, 1918
>
> Dear Mother,
>
> I am still a student at the Infantry Tactics School at Gondrecourt and am learning a great deal on ways to beat the Boche. As a platoon commander who

is responsible for the lives of 60 men, I feel I should learn all I can to properly lead them in battle and save as many lives as possible.

There are always a number of dumb men in every organization and they are the ones whom a commander must especially take care of—the ones who take off their gas masks too soon or stick their heads over the trench parapet at the wrong time and get killed. The responsibility for properly instructing my men and requiring their strict obedience to my orders has been driven home to me while at this Army school.

Your devoted son,
Lem

P.S. Remember me to Maggie [the family cook]. Tell her I am looking forward to eating her delicious waffles and hot rolls for breakfast when I get home. LCS

French General Henri Pétain, the hero of Verdun, inspected the 2nd Battalion at the end of training. The battalion formed in the streets of Menacourt at 7:00 a.m., where it stood in ranks until 4:00 p.m. awaiting Pétain's arrival. The Marines in their forest green uniforms apparently impressed him. He was heard to remark to General Pershing, "I am very impressed with the military bearing of your regiment of Marines. It is obvious they are like our Chasseur Alpine troops, the elite corps of the French Army."[7]

Shepherd returned to Menacourt, and the Blue Devils returned to the trenches. As they left, their band played "The Star-Spangled Banner." Late in September, Shepherd's platoon boarded troop trains for transport to the Bourmont training area, the headquarters of the U.S. Army's 2nd Division (regulars), which included the 4th Marine Brigade.

Bourmont-Damblain Training Area, September 1917–May 1918

Late in October the 5th Marines were moved to the Bourmont training area, where it was organized into the 4th Marine Brigade, consisting of the 5th and 6th Marine Regiments and the 6th Machine Gun Battalion, approximately 9,444 officers and men. Together with the 9th and 23rd Infantry Regiments, 2nd Field Artillery Brigade, 2nd Engineer

Regiment, and various service troops, it made up the U.S. Army's 2nd Division (regulars).

Shortly after the battalion's arrival in the small village of Damblain, the troops were quartered in wooden-frame, tar-paper-covered buildings without floors and heated by only two small wood-burning stoves. Shepherd was billeted on the second story of a small French buvette (part bar, part restaurant, part café) called the Café du Garre because it was located beside a railroad spur that connected Damblain with the main railroad line. The living quarters of the proprietor and his wife were adjacent to the room used for the café. There was a hall stairway between the two rooms leading to Shepherd's quarters on the second floor. The officers' mess was in a stone building a few doors away. The other companies of the battalion were billeted throughout the village. As in most French provincial villages, the streets were unpaved and there was no running water or toilet facilities. The companies dug their own latrines and hauled water in water carts from the village pump.[8]

The weather turned cold and bitter. The winter rains quickly turned to snow. Wise shrugged off the weather, however, and put the battalion through the final grind of heavy training until the men were tough as nails. Shepherd remembered that he quickly got damn sick of the place. The battalion was constantly on alert. Sometimes at night the men were called out without warning to hike in subzero weather. One night about midnight the call to arms sounded, whereupon each man was issued a bandoleer of ammunition and the battalion moved out. After a march of about four miles brought them to the town of Brouains, the battalion was inspected by the regimental commander. On the return march, Shepherd's feet began to hurt. When he returned to his billet and took off his boots, he found that he had put the right boot on his left foot and the left boot on his right foot. The English boots he was wearing were broad in the toes, and in his befogged condition in the semidarkness, he had not noticed the mistake. He learned later that the two battalion commanders of the 5th Marines had been dining with the regimental commander that evening and that each began bragging about who had the better battalion. In order to decide the argument, the regimental commander told them to turn out their battalions in heavy marching order and march to Brouains, where he would inspect them. Shepherd said that he never forgot that night march. Around Christmas they marched to some mock trenches, where they spent three days in simulated trench warfare. It was rugged duty, but it toughened the men up.[9]

It was during this time that Shepherd found out a little more about his battalion commander, who was regarded as something of an ogre. One night when he stood duty as the OD (officer of the day), he had to break up a fight between some French and American soldiers in a small café. He sent the Americans to their billets, but he had to call out the guard to remove the French. The woman who owned the café accused Shepherd of ruining her trade. She got so mad that she fell on the floor and started gnawing on the rung of a chair. The OD had orders to report anything out of the ordinary to Colonel Wise, so at about 10:00 p.m. Shepherd went to his quarters. Wise listened to the story, complimented him on his handling of the incident, and then told him to sit down, since he wanted to talk to him. Shepherd rather hesitantly took the indicated chair and listened intently as Wise gave him a fatherly talk. Wise admitted to being an old SOB but said it was for a reason. He was trying to get the battalion ready for combat, and that required instant obedience to orders and carrying them out to the best of their ability. Shepherd remembered the talk for the rest of his life. It was the only time Wise ever showed another side of himself, the only time he explained that he had a purpose for being the way he was.[10]

While in Damblain, Shepherd acquired a shaggy little dog he named Kiki after a famous French actress. The dog was a mixed breed, part beagle and part terrier, with long, white hair and several patches of black. Kiki became Shepherd's companion and followed him everywhere, even sleeping at the foot of his bed at night. He grew to love the dog as it was the first real pet he had ever had. The two became inseparable.[11]

Paris Sojourn

In late November, Wise authorized a few officers liberty in Paris. Shepherd and a buddy jumped at the chance. They left Damblain on a Friday afternoon, hiked five miles to the train station, and arrived in

Paris at about 11:00 a.m. on Saturday. The two drew back pay and set out to see the city and do a little shopping. The stores were packed with beautiful things, and there were lots of pretty girls everywhere. That evening they went to a nightclub called the Folies Bergère and had a great time. Shepherd had never seen anything like it.[12]

Shepherd's mother encouraged him to visit the historic buildings and monuments in Paris if he ever visited the city. He tried to outsmart her by buying a packet of tourist postcards, hiring a taxi, and driving around the city. At each point of interest, he stuck his head out the window of the cab, looked at the building, and pressed on to the next one. At the end of an hour, he had covered all the points of interest in downtown Paris. He sent the packet to his mother, proclaiming that he had visited all the historic buildings in the packet.

That night Shepherd ran into several friends and partied all night. When he woke up the next morning, he panicked when he found that his train was due to leave in 15 minutes. He jumped into his clothes, dashed to the clerk's office, paid for the room, and caught a taxi for the railroad station. The train was just pulling out. He sprinted to the steps of the last coach, made a spectacular flying leap, and climbed aboard. He caught his breath, heaved a sigh of relief, and took a seat by the window. As he looked out, he observed several of his fellow officers on the other train just pulling out. He panicked! The conductor came by, looked at his ticket, and told him that he was on the wrong train! Shepherd got directions from the conductor, and after a roundabout trip that involved changing trains and a forced march, he finally arrived back at Damblain at six in the morning. It was a harrowing experience, as the thought of having to face Wise's tongue-lashing sent shivers down his spine!

CHAPTER 5

The Blooding, March–May 1918

The battalion was in the final stages of its training program, and after the months of field training, everyone was anxious to go to the front. The 1st Division (regulars) had gone into the trenches south of Verdun in January, and there were persistent rumors that another division would soon follow. In early March 1918 the 2nd Division, including the 5th Marines, received orders for movement to a quiet section of the front. Prior to the move, there was a change of command in the 55th Company. Captain Butler was succeeded by Captain Blanchfield, who had been the Marine gunner of the company. Due to his years of service, he had been promoted to temporary captain ahead of the lieutenants in the company. The company had been in France since the previous June, and after the long months of intensive training, everyone was anxious to get into combat. Both officers and enlisted men had come to France to help win the war, and they were all eager to get on with it.

In the late afternoon on Friday, March 13, the company loaded on a standard French troop train and departed for the front. The train was composed of small freight cars, each marked *40 Hommes and 8 Chevaux*, with flat cars for transport and a second-class coach for the officers. Since the American infantry companies included more men than those of the French, the troops were packed into the freight cars like sardines in a tin can. No allowance had been made to accommodate the greater size of an American unit. The following morning, March 14, the company detrained at the shell-torn village of Dugay, 20 miles southwest of Verdun, and marched to a well-camouflaged cantonment a short distance from the front, the site of a savage bloodbath in 1916. Shepherd observed that the ground in this area was pockmarked with shell holes resulting from German artillery fire during the four years of fighting that had taken place around Verdun. The countless shell holes were filled with stagnant water, and those that had been made by mustard gas shells were covered by a yellow scum. Together with the many shattered tree stumps and discarded equipment, the holes gave the area a war-torn, depressing appearance.

Frontline Duty

That night the battalion took over the frontline trenches of the Montgermont quiet sector until March 28. While moving up, the battalion came under a light bombardment for the first time. The first casualty occurred at the train station. The first two rounds were uncomfortably close but did not cause any casualties. The third round came whistling in and landed in the middle of the 5th Regiment's band equipment, causing one casualty. A piece of shrapnel pierced the base drum, earning the instrument the right to wear a wound stripe. Shepherd recalled that he would never forget the excitement at being in contact with the enemy after months of training and anticipation. He exclaimed, "Here is the real war, and I am in it."[1]

Generally, the trench system consisted of three parallel trenches. The forward trench looked out into no-man's-land, the unoccupied ground between the two sides. Sentries cautiously peered out into this desolate, forlorn, shell-churned ground. Demolished and half-destroyed houses and villages often dotted the landscape.

No-man's-land varied from sector to sector, sometimes placing enemy soldiers within talking distance and sometimes stretching to more than a kilometer. Multiple belts of barbed wire, frequently 150 feet or more in depth, lined the ground in front of the trench. The wire was covered by rifles and interlocking bands of machine gun fire to create a crossfire.

Light artillery, the famous French 75, was positioned within a mile or so of the front line. The heavy artillery—the 155-mm howitzers and guns—was further back. Carefully constructed fire plans called for the delivery of standing barrages in front of any threatened point. Patrols going forward of the line could be covered by curtain and box barrages if they ran into trouble.

A support trench behind the front line served as a secondary defense position, as well as offering additional shelter and protection against shellfire. A third "reserve" trench could be as much as several miles behind the first two. Communication trenches served as protected avenues of approach among the three systems.

The 55th Company entered a shallow communication trench in single file, heavy marching order on their backs, rifles slung over their shoulders, and gas masks on alert. The trench deepened—up to their waist—cutting right and then left, zigzag—to contain the impact of a lucky shell. Mud-caked shoes made it difficult to walk in the slime. It stuck to uniforms, equipment, and, despite their best efforts, smeared weapons with a claylike muck. A foul stench hung in the air, which many veterans recognized instantly as the cloying stench of long-dead bodies.

Although the Montgermont sector was quiet, every night there were patrols and wiring parties. Several times these parties made contact with German patrols. There was also intermittent machine gun fire at night and an occasional bombardment, especially on rear positions and communications trenches. The Marines gained valuable experience, especially in organizing a position and patrolling in darkness.

The following morning Shepherd received orders to conduct a reconnaissance that night of the frontline sector that was to be occupied by the 55th Company. About dusk he and another officer from the battalion were led by a guide to the command post of the French battalion they were to relieve. Under the light of a flickering candle, they were shown a map that was marked with both the French and German trenches—the French in red ink and the German in blue. Following a brief discussion, a French major led them through a maze of communication and support trenches to an observation post in the frontline trench. Shepherd remarked later that he experienced a thrill of excitement. He was fascinated looking out into the desolation of no-man's-land by the light of constant star shell illumination. It was the practice of both the Allied and French troops occupying the frontline trenches to fire star shells or Very pistol flares whenever a suspicious sound was heard or movement detected in no-man's-land. The two Marines returned to their lines just before dawn and, after a couple hours of sleep and some breakfast, they conducted a brief on what they had learned.[2]

The relief took place without incident the following night, and by dawn Shepherd's platoon were well established. In the daylight, he could clearly see the German trenches several hundred yards away. At long last he was in contact with the enemy, which gave him a feeling of satisfaction. The French guide pointed out a large hill mass where thousands of men had been killed during the early months of the war. There was still a stench in the air from the unburied bodies when the wind blew in their direction.

The company soon fell into the usual trench routine. Following morning "stand-to," inspection, and breakfast, the men undertook any number of chores, ranging from cleaning latrines to filling sandbags or repairing duckboards. During daylight hours, they conducted all work below ground and away from the snipers' searching rifles. Those not on duty slept in dugouts in the frontline and supporting trenches. Those dugouts were only a few feet underground and were little more than splinter-proof shelters. Entrances were covered by a heavy blanket to protect against gas attack. Unfortunately, they kept out fresh air and sunlight, which made the dugouts cold and damp, as no fires were permitted and the only light was a flickering candle. Inside the dugouts there were several tiers of wooden bunks covered with straw-filled sacks that were used for mattresses.

Shepherd's No-Man's-Land Patrol

A few days after the company took over the trenches, Shepherd was told by the battalion intelligence officer, 1st Lieutenant Samuel Calvin Cumming, that he had been designated to lead a reconnaissance patrol into no-man's-land to capture a German prisoner. Shepherd was excited and anxious at the same time. This was the first Marine patrol to go into no-man's-land, and he was determined to prove himself. He sat down with Cumming and went over all the intelligence that was available, and they talked at length to gather all the information that was available on the German troops occupying the sector. He then went to a forward observation post to study the terrain and to plan the patrol's route.[3]

He selected 15 of the best men in his platoon for the patrol and rehearsed several formations to use for this duty from among the men in the platoon and rehearsed several formations to be taken on signal—

> one a "V" during our advance across no-man's-land, another for encircling the German listening post I had selected to raid and a third for the withdrawal of the patrol if we ran into an enemy ambush. One of the patrol was detailed as the "get-away" in the event the latter situation was encountered. I also checked the equipment of the men to insure no one was carrying any article which might rattle and that all weapons were in good firing condition. In addition to our normal arms, every man carried a trench knife and wire cutters. One man made himself a stout club from a small tree root [into] which he drove nails so that the pointed ends protruded. We were truly "armed to the teeth."[4]
>
> About midnight we blackened our faces with burnt cork, checked on the password for the night and leaving the front line trench worked our way through the labyrinth of barbed wire by a path which had been pointed out.
>
> Once the patrol was clear of the wire we assumed a "V" formation and began a stealthy advance across No Man's Land in the direction of the German trenches. In the darkness every stump looked like a German and when we observed several man-like objects which appeared to be moving we were sure it was a hostile patrol. On signal my patrol fanned out and charged with bayonets fixed. Much to my chagrin the moving objects turned out to be a clump of bushes swaying in the light wind.
>
> After further advance the patrol arrived in close proximity to the German outpost I had selected to raid. We crawled up to the surrounding barbed wire entanglement, quietly cut a path through the enemy wire and charged the position. To our surprise and disappointment, we discovered the outpost was unoccupied. Reforming my patrol, I decided we had had enough for the night and we returned to our lines.[5]
>
> On arrival at the barbed wire entanglements in front of our trenches, I searched for the opening. In the mass of wire, it was difficult to find it. After several unsuccessful attempts, I finally led the patrol under the wire, cutting the strands we were able to crawl underneath. It was close to daylight when we finally reached our trenches.

After submitting his report to Captain Butler, he turned in, completely exhausted physically and mentally from the night's activities.

The battalion spent two weeks in the frontline trenches and then moved to a reserve area near Fort Douaumont, the largest and highest fort on the ring of 19 large defensive works protecting the city of Verdun. The fort fell to the Germans early in 1916 but was retaken before the year was out. Shepherd was impressed with the fort's massive masonry construction and labyrinth of tunnels.

The last days of May brought welcome relief for the men of the Marine brigade. Warm weather had finally arrived, giving them an opportunity to shed their long winter underwear and dry out after an onerous tour of duty in the trenches. Trench life was challenging, and living in them was awful. The men were surrounded by dirt and the food was poor. They had to contend with constant alerts, occasional shelling, rats, and no one washed for days, even weeks. But on May 30, they got a welcome surprise, a rare day off to celebrate Decoration Day. For most it was a time of rest and relaxation—a relief from the constant training regimen. It was a time to write letters, catch up on sleep, or, for a lucky few, go on a date with a local jeune fille. Lem Shepherd was one of the fortunate ones. He had met "an attractive French girl" and had been invited to dinner at her home—along with a host of relatives, who wanted to look him over. In preparation for the big event, he was "squaring away" his best uniform. To his great disappointment, at four o'clock that afternoon, May 30, the battalion received orders to pack up and stand by for boarding camions. He knew the camions meant action. Camions were French army trucks that were notorious for being uncomfortable. They carried 20 to 25 men who sat on narrow wooden seats along each side and another in the middle. The wheels were solid rubber, which jostled the men mercilessly on the pothole-filled roads. The camions were driven by Annamite drivers, two to a truck, uniformed in khaki and crested helmets. There would be no dinner. All he could do was send his orderly with a note of apology to Marianne. Thus ended what could have developed into a budding romance.[6]

Lieutenant Colonel Wise was in Paris with his wife, a volunteer nurse. They were enjoying the hospitality of a family friend. His relaxation was interrupted abruptly by a telephone call. "My adjutant, Lieutenant James Hennen Legendre, told me, 'We've been ordered up to the front at once. The Germans have broken through and are headed for Paris.' 'I'll be there,' I told him."[7]

Wise got back just in time. "The bugle sounded 'assembly,' and the battalion fell in on the road alongside the camions. Platoon leaders' whistles blew and the men climbed aboard," Wise later said. The vehicle drivers were often French colonial soldiers who drove with reckless abandon, scaring the hell out of their passengers. One officer noted, "Lucky if we don't get killed before reaching the front."[8]

Floyd Gibbons, a well-known correspondent for the *Chicago Tribune*, also was in Paris trying to confirm a rumor that a huge German offensive was bearing down on the "City of Light."[9]

CHAPTER 6

Bois de la Brigade de Marine (Belleau Wood), May 31–June 5, 1918

On March 21, 1918, the Germans launched their last great offensive on the Western Front from La Fere to Arras, defended by the British Army. The attack seemed unstoppable. There were not enough British and French reserves to plug the gap in the lines where the Germans broke through. A hurried call went out on the afternoon of May 30 to the inexperienced American 2nd Division to "march to the sound of the guns." A French general worried that *les Américains* could not hold and said as much to Colonel Preston Brown, the 2nd Division chief of staff. Brown indignantly replied, "General, these are American regulars. In a hundred and fifty years they have never been defeated. They will hold!"[1]

The massive 14-mile convoy carrying the 2nd Division—28 thousand men and seven thousand horses—headed in the direction of Paris. As they neared the city and could see the church spires on its outskirts, speculation ran high on the possibility that by some stroke of good fortune the battalion would be given liberty in this alluring city. Their hopes were soon shattered, however, as the convoy passed around the environs of Paris, which soon faded in the distance. The convoy continued along the Paris–Metz highway toward Château-Thierry."[2]

Finally, around four o'clock that afternoon, the convoy stopped and let the troops off. Then the marching started toward the front, while the French refugees were going the other way. It was the first time Marines had witnessed the human cost of the war. They met streams of peasants traveling south. Many were in horse-drawn carts filled with their household belongings. Some of the women were rolling baby carriages or wheelbarrows loaded with personal effects. Intermingled with the refugees were French ambulatory soldiers and other wounded in ambulances. Occasionally, the column was passed by French cavalry, with lances in hand, headed toward the front, or a staff car transporting anxious-looking French officers.[3]

About midnight, the battalion halted and bivouacked in an open field close to Pyramid Farm in Marigny-en-Orxois, in the north of France in the township of Château-Thierry. They were so tired that no one even bothered to take off his bedroll; they just collapsed on their packs. A French battalion of 75-mm guns was emplaced in a field close by and fired constantly during the night. The sharp crack of the guns was earsplitting and permitted the troops little sleep.

In the morning, Shepherd sent out a foraging detail, which returned with several rabbits and chickens they had liberated from a deserted farmyard. He had barely finished breakfast when the battalion was ordered to fall in and march toward its defensive sector on the Paris–Metz Road, nine miles north and west of Château-Thierry. A signpost by the side of the road pointed to the right—Paris 65 kilometers.[4]

In less than an hour, the battalion reached a narrow dirt road, its defensive position. From one end to the other, the sector stretched over four kilometers, about two and a half miles. The extended frontage forced Wise to place all four companies on line, around 1,000 men—18th Company on the extreme left, in the northeast corner of the Bois de Veuilly; 43rd Company next in line; 55th Company in and around Les Mares farm; and the 51st Company on the right flank, south of Hill 142. The ground was open on their right front, gradually sloping upward to a wooded hill (Hill 165) about half a mile away. Les Mares farm stood on their left front, while a checkerboard pattern of woods and fields swung away from them on both sides.[5]

The 55th Company was halted on the crest of a hill and moved into a clump of woods for concealment from German artillery observation while the officers went forward to make a detailed reconnaissance of the ground. By now the company was coming within range of the German artillery, and an occasional shell fell close by.

As Blanchfield and Shepherd left the shelter of the trees, a German artillery barrage drove the last of the French soldiers from the field. Explosions and bursts of flame marked the German's steady advance over the scarred terrain. The retreating poilus withdrew in good order.

The two Americans had seen enough and returned to the woods. Shepherd waited patiently for the order to move forward, but Blanchfield was overwhelmed by the tactical situation. The older man seemed paralyzed with indecision. Captain Blanchfield could not read a map and seemed helplessly bewildered in the fast-moving situation. Since Shepherd was the senior first lieutenant in the company, he turned his platoon over to his gunnery sergeant and remained with Blanchfield in order to assist him to direct the platoons into their designated defense sectors. There were no prepared defenses and no time to wait for "proper" entrenching tools. The men were ordered to dig foxholes, which were nothing more than little scooped-up hollows similar to a grave but about a foot deep, with earth piled up in front for a parapet. They broke out small T-handle shovels. Others used anything at hand—bayonets, mess kits, spoons—to dig up the rich farmland.[6]

Les Mares Farm

The 55th Company occupied a position just north of the tiny village of Champillon, in an area called Belleau Wood. Its right flank tied in with the 51st Company on the Champillon–Torcy Road, and its left flank was in and around Les Mares farm, using the imposing, red-roofed farmhouse, with its surrounding three-foot stone wall, and barn as part of the defensive position. Shepherd ordered his platoon to defend the Les Mares farmhouse and its adjoining barnyard and the remainder of the company to dig in along several hundred yards of assigned frontage. The farm stood on rising ground, dotted with clumps of woods, with wheat fields here and there, and tall hedges.[7]

Initially, the U.S. 2nd Division units were attached to the French 43rd and 164th Divisions. Taking position as they arrived on the field and thinly spread on a front of 15 kilometers, soldiers of the 3rd Brigade were split on both flanks, with Marines of the 4th Brigade in the center.

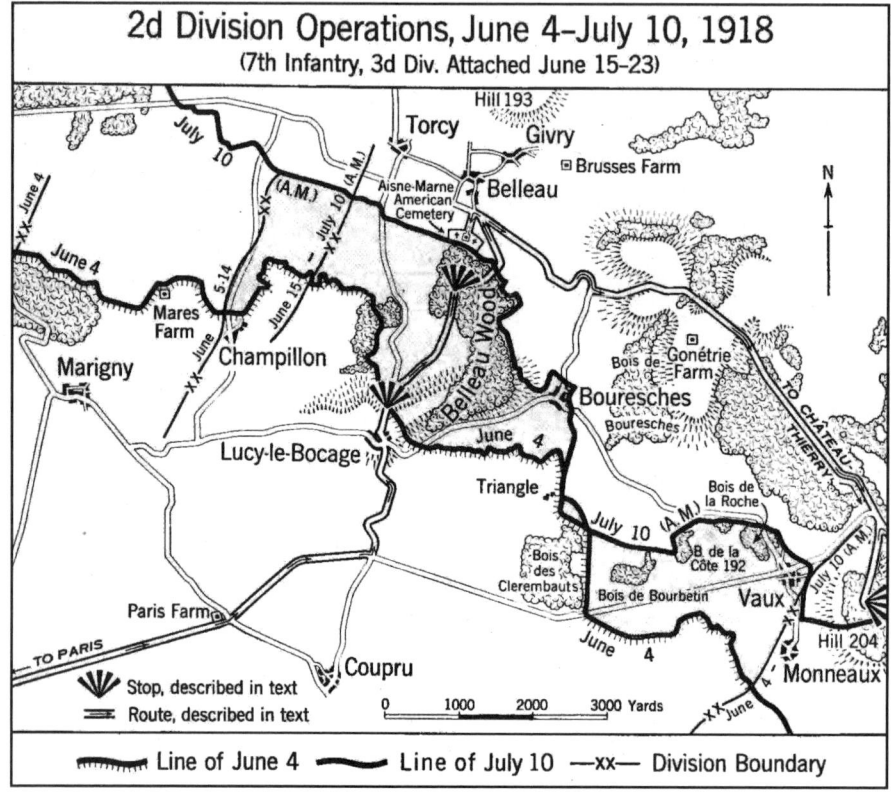

The 2nd Engineers operations at Belleau Woods. (Colonel William Anderson)

On June 3, the last exhausted rear guard French elements withdrew and regrouped behind the line formed by the Marines and soldiers of the 2nd Division. During the evening of June 3, the Marines of the 2nd Battalion, 5th Marines, repulsed the attack of the German 273rd Reserve Infantry Regiment, 197th Division, at Les Mares; this would be as close as the German army would get to Paris for the remainder of the war.

By late afternoon, Shepherd could see the advancing German infantry on the distant horizon. Their supporting artillery was dropping shells in the area of Les Mares farm. He recalled having an uncomfortable feeling that within hours the surging German attack would be upon them.

The advance of the German troops. (American Battle Monuments Commission)

CHAPTER 7

Wounded in Action, June 1918

There was little enemy activity during the night. The next morning, June 3, Shepherd took out a patrol to reconnoiter a small knoll about three hundred yards in front of the lines that offered excellent observation. He recommended to Blanchfield that it be used as an outpost. Blanchfield concurred, and Shepherd led a squad, with a light machine gun, under a sergeant, to the outpost with orders to open fire when the enemy came within range and withdraw when the Germans closed in.[1]

The German shelling increased, signaling an infantry assault. Shepherd could see thin lines of German infantry advancing. He worried about the men in the outpost. It was isolated and could get cut off. He went to Blanchfield and requested to check on the small detachment. Blanchfield quickly agreed, although by now a heavy concentration of shellfire was falling over the area. Shepherd later admitted that he didn't know why he suggested it because his men had orders to withdraw when they could no longer hold the position. He wanted a personal look at their situation, however. He and his orderly started across the field. Shells were exploding close by. One fell six feet to his right, covering him with dirt, but fortunately it was a dud. When they reached the outpost, his men were shooting at the German infantry from foxholes they had dug on the forward slope of the hill. Shepherd took cover behind a tree just behind the crest. Suddenly, a bullet from a German machine gun hit him in the neck. It was a glancing blow, but the force of impact turned him half around, and he dropped to the ground. His first thought was that the bullet had gone through his throat. He recalled spitting into his hand to see if he was bleeding internally. To his surprise, there was no blood. The bullet had only creased the side of his neck, passing within half an inch of his jugular vein. It tore away part of his collar, taking the Marine emblem with it.

The Germans began encircling the outpost, and rifle and machine-gun fire increased in intensity. He crawled up beside his men, one of whom had been seriously wounded, but the rest kept firing, until just after dark, when he gave the order to withdraw to the front line, bringing the wounded man with them. Shepherd refused to be evacuated and had the company corpsman dress the wound; later that night he went back to the rear to have it properly bandaged.[2] Shepherd returned to France in 1919 and visited the knoll where he was wounded and found the tree he had been leaning against. He was amazed to find the trunk of the tree with seven bullet holes in it about the height of his head.

Shepherd was awarded the Navy Cross, the Army Distinguished Service Cross, and the Croix de Guerre for the action at the outpost:

> For extraordinary heroism while serving with the Fifth Regiment (Marines), 2d Division, A.E.F., in action on 3 June 1918, near the Lucy-Torcy Roads, France. First Lieutenant Shepherd declined medical treatment after being wounded and continued courageously to lead his men.

In receiving the award, Shepherd commented, "I have always felt I did no more than what is expected of a United States Marine."

First Blood

The Germans' attack was stopped, and for the next two days they continued to probe but did not directly assault the Marine defensive line. On June 4, however, Marine snipers detected movement in the field of waist-high wheat in front of the lines. Gunnery Sergeant David L. Buford led a hastily organized patrol toward the spot and surprised the German patrol. Buford, who was a wonderful pistol shot, killed seven Germans with his automatic pistol. The remaining men of the German patrol jumped up and ran toward their own lines, but several were killed and wounded by the Marine snipers. That stopped the infiltration in the area. It was the first bodily contact with the enemy, and it gave the Marines a feeling of satisfaction and confidence to have routed the enemy in this brief engagement with German troops. The patrol brought back the bodies of the dead Germans, and it was determined they were from a Jäger unit. The battalion intelligence officer, First Lieutenant Bill Matthews, was delighted to obtain the identification of the opposing unit. One of the dead Germans had a silver coin in his pocket, which Shepherd kept as a souvenir of the occasion.[3]

On the evening of June 6, the 2nd Battalion was relieved of its frontline duties by a French unit and assembled in a wooded area in the rear of its old position. It was pitch black [when] they began a lateral march through a dense woods. The march turned out to be a nightmare. Contact was maintained by each man holding on to the bayonet scabbard of the man to his front. The battalion wandered around the woods for hours until it reached a point between two high banks where the terrain opened up into sloping grain fields. Belleau Wood was on their right flank.

Firing broke out at the head of the column. Shepherd was near the rear of the column when he received word to "about face to the rear." They had been taught never to march to the rear without determining who gave the order. Since the 55th Company was the last in the column, Captain Blanchfield passed the word forward asking who had given the order. By the time the word came back that Wise had given the order, machine-gun bullets had erupted from the woods around them.[4]

Dawn was just breaking, and Shepherd could see Germans moving in the clump of woods to the front and in an extended wooded area on the right. Wise had unwittingly led the battalion into an open field on the left side of Belleau Wood that was heavily defended by the Germans. The firefight continued with intensity. German *miniwerfer* shells landed with a dull thud and exploded with a tremendous concussion that was truly frightening. After checking the disposition of his men, Shepherd took position on the edge of the woods, where he could direct their fire toward the enemy to the front.

The 55th Company was now in the lead when suddenly several German machine guns opened fire. Shepherd got word from a runner that Captain Blanchfield had been killed along the side of the road.

Shepherd continued getting the platoons in position along the edge of the woods. Fire was coming from a little clump of woods to his front and also from Belleau Wood on the right. Suddenly, his orderly cried out and went down with a Mauser slug in his leg. Shepherd was bending down to help the Marine when something walloped him in the left thigh just below the hip; it felt like the kick of a mule. He crumpled in a heap, unable to move, not realizing that he had been hit. He glanced down and saw the bullet that had struck him. Blood oozed from his trousers. His pet dog Kiki, who had loyally followed, was on the ground beside him, his head on Shepherd's leg. He was so quiet Shepherd thought he was dead. He picked him up and threw him off his leg, but the dog jumped up and ran right back to him. Shepherd was elated that his dog was unhurt.[5]

Shepherd and Martin were evacuated to an aid station and given emergency treatment before being placed in an ambulance and transported to Hospital Number One. The field hospital was in a schoolhouse with French mathematical figures still on the blackboard; the school had been hurriedly dismissed a few days earlier on the approach of the Germans. The pews and desks had been removed and litter racks had taken their place, each with its blanket-draped litter. A portion of the schoolroom had been partitioned off by means of blankets into a resuscitation ward where the heat from several Primus stoves were going full blast. Shepherd was lying on a stretcher when a medic told him that he couldn't take the dog with him. Shepherd told him that they could leave him or take him and the dog. The medic relented, and the dog shared the stretcher.[6]

Shepherd was taken outside and loaded into one of a long, seemingly unbroken line of muddy ambulances. The interior of the vehicle held four litters, two above and two below, suspended from hooks. As soon as it was loaded an orderly motioned to the Annamite (Vietnamese) driver and, with a gnashing of gears, the vehicle lurched forward, out of the yard. The solid rubber tires jolted over the rough road. The wounded groaned with pain. Shepherd swore that the driver went out of his way to hit every pothole and rough spot. After what seemed to be an eternity, the ambulance reached Red Cross Hospital Number Two in Paris.

Shepherd stayed there 10 days and then was transferred to another hospital to make room for more wounded.

Shepherd was still in his disheveled, muddy field uniform, complete with bloodstained trousers and blouse with the collar shot away. The doctor gave him permission to go into the city to buy a new uniform and toilet articles—if he could walk on crutches. Shepherd assured him that he was an expert, which was a stretch, because he had never been on crutches before! It was midafternoon when he left the hospital. He took a taxi into the Place de l'Opéra. His appearance must have startled the chic Parisians as he hobbled along on his crutches with Kiki on a chain beside him. He was still wearing his steel helmet, and his uniform was covered with mud. The high collar of the coat was badly torn where the bullet had struck his neck, and his breeches were caked with blood from the wound in his leg.[7]

As luck would have it, he ran into another officer from his company, who had been gassed. The two decided to extend their liberty and have dinner before turning in. As the night wore on, Shepherd's leg started giving him fits, and he grew faint with pain. He caught a taxi to the hospital gate, which was a quarter mile to his tent. He had a heck of time making it back—he was so faint that he had to stop and lean against the fence every few minutes. His sojourn had caused infection to set in, and his temperature rose to 104 degrees. He was immediately wheeled into the operating room for emergency surgery. Gangrene developed in the wound, and when he woke up the next morning he was lying on his back with Dakin's solution tubes in his leg. He couldn't turn over because he had seven rubber tubes in the wound, which had been opened up so the Dakin's solution could drain through and come out the back side where the bullet had gone through. He lay there for three weeks without turning over in the hard bed![8]

The French had a big Fourth of July parade and, as a courtesy to the United States, invited a platoon from each battalion of the 2nd Division to participate. Shepherd was well enough to go into Paris for this event and was standing on the edge of the sidewalk at the Place de la Concorde watching the troops pass when he saw his former platoon from the 55th Company. In his enthusiasm he hobbled out on his crutches and marched with them for a short distance. He was thrilled to be with the men of his former platoon again, or what was left of them after the heavy casualties suffered in Belleau Wood.

For his heroism at Belleau Wood, the 21-year-old Shepherd received the Army Distinguished Service Cross, the Navy Cross, and the French Croix de Guerre.

Shepherd was transferred to another hospital, and in the latter part of August he convinced the doctors that he was fit for duty, after Fritz Wise requested his return as soon as he was physically able, as he needed the services of his former officers to rebuild his organization. In the process of returning to the 5th Marines, Shepherd's faithful dog disappeared. He never saw the dog again. "He was a faithful and lovable pooch."

CHAPTER 8

Saint-Mihiel All-American Offensive, September 10–16, 1918

Shepherd spent several days traveling from one replacement depot to another before rejoining a much changed 55th Company. None of the former officers remained, and only a few of the enlisted men were still in ranks. Casualties in Belleau Wood and at Soissons had taken a toll. Shortly after his return on September 4, the battalion received orders to the Saint-Mihiel salient. It marched about 20 kilometers each night toward the zone of action and bivouacked in the woods during the day. The weather was cold and rainy, and the long hikes, which Shepherd was not physically conditioned for, caused the wound in his leg to pain him considerably during the 10 nights of marching toward the front.[1]

On September 10, the battalion finally reached the small shell-torn village of Limey, which was barely recognizable as a former town. Four years of war had enabled the French to dig a complex and extensive trench system and install masses of barbed wire in front of their lines. Heavy rains had left the trenches ankle deep in mud, which slowed the troops from reaching their jump-off positions.

The Saint-Mihiel offensive, the first all-American offensive of the war, began at 1:00 a.m. on September 12 with a tremendous artillery barrage. Shepherd recalled that the 55th Company formed up in an old French trench until ten o'clock, when it "went over the top." He had anticipated that the company would experience difficulty in passing through the extended barbed wire entanglements, but artillery fires and the Bangalore Torpedoes had cut lanes through the wire that made the passage fairly easy. Once in the clear the attack progressed rather rapidly

The downed German plane from which Shepherd and other Marines snagged souvenirs. (Public Domain)

since only light resistance was initially encountered—the Germans had recently withdrawn the bulk of their troops in order to shorten their lines after the reverses suffered at Château-Thierry and Soissons.[2]

On the first day of the attack, the 6th Marines who made the initial assault were followed by the 5th Marines, who leapfrogged and continued the attack. The 2nd Battalion followed the 9th Infantry. The division captured the Corps' objective and dug in on a broad plateau, over seven kilometers from the line of departure. The next afternoon, September 13, the 2nd Battalion was in support, occupying a ravine in the southern edge of the Bois de Fey, remaining there until the night of September 15. It was here that Shepherd observed a German plane pass directly over the battalion at a very low altitude. Immediately everyone began firing at the German plane. In the excitement of the moment, he drew his pistol and joined in. Minutes later, the plane crashed in front of the lines. The men swarmed around the wreckage, which was practically intact and only slightly damaged. The pilot was dead. In minutes the plane was completely stripped by souvenir hunters. Shepherd retrieved the aviator's bloodstained goggles, the plane's altimeter, and a piece of the wing covering with its Iron Cross marking. The incident was an exciting event and served to encourage the men to fire at low-flying enemy planes whenever they came near.[3]

On September 16, the battalion was relieved and, after a series of night marches, bivouacked in a small town where the company joined a number of officers and a replacement draft bringing it up to a combat strength of 250 men. The older veterans knew this signaled immediate action. On September 29 the company received an order to stand by for camions, which arrived at 6:00 p.m., arriving about midnight at a shell-torn village where the men were billeted.[4]

CHAPTER 9

Blanc Mont (White Mountain), October 1–9, 1918

Shepherd's Worst Day of the War, October 4, 1918

The 2nd Division was assigned to capture Blanc Mont—"White Mountain"—the name deriving from the chalky nature of the ground. It was a heavily fortified position and commanding terrain that had been held by the Germans since 1914. It was one of the critical points of the Hindenburg Line.[1]

Shepherd believed they really didn't have it that bad at Mihiel, but Blanc Mont was another story. As far as he was concerned October 3 at Blanc Mont was the toughest day of the war.

Blanc Mont was the scene of heavy fighting throughout the war. During 1916 the Germans had strengthened their defenses with a series of concrete emplacements in depth, covering every avenue of approach with dugouts a hundred feet deep, large enough to house whole companies of reserve troops.

On October 2, the night before the attack, Shepherd was called to regimental headquarters and was informed by Colonel Logan Feland that his platoon would be temporarily assigned as a liaison unit between the 4th Marine Brigade and the 3rd Army Brigade. Major General John A. Lejeune, USMC, had succeeded Major General James Harbord in command of the 2nd Division. In planning the attack on Blanc Mont, the division's scheme of maneuver called for the 4th Marine Brigade to assault the German position by a frontal attack while the 3rd Army Brigade executed a flanking attack from the right. It was General Lejeune's hope to bypass a large portion of the German defenses.

Shepherd's mission required him to maintain physical contact with the two units and send back hourly reports on their progress. He confessed he was unhappy with the assignment as it required his platoon to advance through the center of the German defenses that the two brigades were bypassing. The assignment spoke volumes about Shepherd's professional reputation for tactical competence: Out of 36 platoon commanders in the 5th Marines, he was singled out, a mark of achievement.[2]

The attack kicked off with a thunderous artillery barrage, blanketing the frontline German trenches with high explosives. The shelling forced them to remain in their concrete bombproofs as the Marines advanced across no-man's-land. Shepherd led his platoon into the maelstrom of exploding shells and small arms fire, keeping fairly close to the zone of action of the 2nd Battalion. He could observe the advancing units of the 3rd Army Brigade in the distance. In the middle of the morning, the 23rd Infantry entered a wooded area and he lost visual contact with their leading troops, so he led his platoon further off the right flank of the 2nd Battalion in order to regain contact.

His platoon could easily be detected by the Germans, as they were advancing over open terrain without any cover, so he decided to let them continue to advance several hundred yards on the right of the 2nd Battalion while he moved across the terrain between the battalion and the 23rd Infantry with a couple of his men, hoping the small group would not be observed by the enemy. The terrain was rolling, with plenty of cover for concealment, but he never knew when he might encounter a German outpost or strongpoint. He took an extremely hazardous risk of either getting the patrol killed or captured, but at the time it seemed to be the only way to carry out his mission. Fortune was with him, and he did not run into any Germans. He was able to make personal contact with the captain of the left flank company of the 23rd Infantry and accurately report their position to Colonel Feland. Not long after he rejoined his platoon, the 5th Marines and 23rd Infantry converged in their attack on Blanc Mont, so he considered the mission to have been accomplished.[3]

At 7:00 a.m. on October 3, following a cold, sleepless night, the 5th Marines received a delayed order to resume the attack as soon as possible.

The 2nd Battalion jumped off as the assault element. Their advance was slowed due to strong resistance from concealed machine gun emplacements to their front and on both flanks. The advance halted at noon for about an hour and then resumed under intense enemy fire before securing the objective. Before the men could dig in, they came under heavy artillery fire. Shepherd could see the guns of a German battery just a few hundred yards distant firing salvo after salvo in rapid succession at point-blank range. The enemy shells practically blew the top off the hill! The impact of the exploding shells was terrific, and the acid fumes from the burning powder were so choking he could scarcely breathe.

Captain Lemuel C. Shepherd Jr., USMC, 1919. (Virginia Military Institute)

The company was forced to withdraw to a wooded area a couple hundred yards to the rear. Casualties had been severe. Out of the 250 men from the 55th Company who had entered the attack two days previously, only 50 men remained. Shepherd and Lieutenant Coroveau were the only officers left. The 2nd Battalion's history noted: "The battle of Blanc Mont is probably the most difficult engagement in which the battalion participated during the entire war. Our losses were unusually heavy in killed and wounded."[4] Shepherd assumed command of the company.

The next morning, Shepherd went over to Coroveau's foxhole and shared a drink of brandy that he carried for emergency purposes. Shepherd had just returned to his hole when an Austrian 77 shell scored a direct hit on Coroveau's position. The lieutenant and his platoon sergeant were killed instantly, and his platoon runner lost both legs and died before he could be evacuated to a first aid station. Shepherd was infuriated! He said it was one of the few times during the war that he "saw red," and he vowed to kill every German he could find![5]

The 55th Company was withdrawn to the former German trenches on the crest of Blanc Mont, where it took up a support position. A new lieutenant by the name of Voss was assigned as Shepherd's second-in-command. In the late afternoon of October 9, the two were standing on the top of Blanc Mont Ridge when, without warning, a shell from an Austrian 77-mm gun landed with a "zip bang" close by and its fragments riddled Lieutenant Voss's stomach. He took the bulk of the fragments, but a small piece of shrapnel struck Shepherd's left leg below the hip. He didn't feel any pain and managed to carry the badly wounded lieutenant to a nearby trench. His leg collapsed just as he was passing Voss to a corpsman. Afterwards he was at a loss as to how he was able to carry Voss after being wounded. The two officers were evacuated in the same ambulance to a field hospital, where Voss died soon after arrival.[6]

The field hospital was overcrowded with casualties. No beds were available, so Shepherd's stretcher was placed on the ground, where he remained until the next morning, when he was operated on. To add insult to injury, the chloroform he received to knock him out made him deathly ill. The shrapnel had struck him midway between the hip and knee, just missing the bone. The surgeon had to cut through both the front and rear side of his leg to locate and extract the fragment. He was lucky the bone was intact. Following surgery, Shepherd was transported by a French hospital train to a girls' convent in the town of Blois, located on the Loire River, that had been turned into a U.S. Army hospital. The hospital staff happened to be from the Deep South, which pleased him to no end.[7]

After several weeks of convalescence, Shepherd convinced the commanding officer of the hospital to grant him leave in Paris with his former VMI roommate, Captain Fielding Robinson, aide-de-camp to Major General Harbord, the 2nd Division commander. Robinson was able to "snag" a deluxe Cadillac staff car. The two officers lived it up, including a night at the Folies Bergère, a cabaret music hall. They extended their stay in the City of Lights after hearing a strong rumor that the armistice was about to be signed. The rumor turned out to be just that, however, and Shepherd returned to the hospital. Shepherd always regretted he was not in Paris on the night of November 10, 1918, when World War I came to a close after four years of fighting.

Shepherd's wound healed, and he requested to rejoin his unit. A medical board convened, and he convinced the board that he was fit for duty. He received orders to the Army Replacement Center at Le Mains, a town near Tours, where he was informed that the 2nd Division was marching into Germany. On the way to rejoin the division, Shepherd stopped at the paymaster's office in Paris, where he learned that he had been promoted to captain, a rank he would hold for the next 14 years! On January 2, 1919, he finally reached the 2nd Division and had the good fortune to be assigned to his old battalion. Since the 55th Company had its full complement of officers, he was attached to the 51st Company and assigned as the battalion range officer. A month later he was reassigned to his old company when its company commander left for the United States. The company officers were new to him, and only a few of the former enlisted men were still with the company. Nevertheless, he was happy to have command of the same company he had gone to France with as a second lieutenant two years previously.[8]

Shepherd's first order of business was to prepare the company for the possibility of renewed combat. The Germans had refused to agree to the terms of the peace accords. Troops in the occupation were alerted and prepared to march on Berlin. They marched up to a mile from the neutral zone with orders to cross it at nine o'clock at night and burn any house that fired on them. Shepherd had the leading company of the 2nd Battalion, which was the advanced guard. He had issued the march order when, at 8:00 p.m., he received word that the Germans had signed on the dotted line and that the company was to return to its billets. There was a general letdown feeling among all hands. The brigade began occupation duty in Germany. Shepherd was surprised how cooperative the German people were. He was billeted with a German family, who treated him well. When he was ordered to brigade headquarters, the family gave him a going-away party.[9]

Shepherd took the opportunity to take two weeks' leave in England and Scotland with a VMI classmate. Upon his return from leave, he was transferred to the headquarters of the Fourth Marine Brigade and assigned as assistant adjutant to Major Charles D. Barrett and unofficial aide-de-camp to General Wendell Neville, the division commander.

Shepherd became close friends with Barrett and credited him with helping him as a counselor and supporter in various duty assignments. He learned a great deal about staff procedures, while thoroughly enjoying his time at headquarters, "living in style." His time with the brigade was cut short when in August 1919 the 2nd Division received orders to return to the United States aboard the SS *George Washington*.[10]

CHAPTER 10

Streets of New York, August 1919

Midway across the Atlantic, the division received authorization from the secretary of the Navy for it to parade through New York City, provided that the majority of the men approved. The five thousand officers and men aboard the ship were polled, and they unanimously approved. Lejeune, the division commander, sent a wireless to Baker with the results, which he approved. The *George Washington* docked at Hoboken on August 3, 1919, and the division moved by train to an Army camp near Garden City, Long Island. At 3:10 p.m. on August 9, the division marched in a victory parade in full battle dress, "starting at the Memorial Arch at Washington Square in lower Manhattan, up the fashionable 5th Avenue to 110th Street at the upper end of Central Park. Led by General Lejeune on a restless charger, some 25,000 fighting men of the Division—marching on foot in sold formations—as hundreds of thousands of excited onlookers cheered and applauded them along the several mile route."[1]

Among the dignitaries in the reviewing stand in front of the public library were Assistant Secretary of the Navy Franklin D. Roosevelt, Naval Chief of Operations Admiral William S. Benson, and Major General George Barnett, commandant of the Marine Corps. Shepherd's mother and sister watched from the reviewing stand as he marched at the head of the Brigade Headquarters Company.

Four days later, the 8,000-strong 4th Brigade arrived at Washington's Union Station by train at 8:00 a.m. There they initially marched to the vicinity of the Capitol building, where they formed a cordon around its grounds and stacked arms. Women from the District of Columbia Chapter Canteen Service, plus field workers of the Potomac Division of the Department of Military Relief, served coffee and iced tea to the Marines as they waited at the Capitol grounds (and, after the parade, coffee and buns).[2]

The parade route was from the Peace Monument (near the Capitol) up Pennsylvania Avenue past President Woodrow Wilson, with the lead elements reaching there at 12:40 p.m. Throngs of cheering and applauding crowds lined the route. Both houses of Congress had adjourned for two hours, and the lunch hour of government workers had been extended so that all could view the last formal appearance of this famous Marine unit prior to it being disbanded at Quantico, Virginia, in early August. During the parade Shepherd's thoughts returned to the march he had made down Pennsylvania Avenue while a cadet at VMI on the occasion of the inauguration of President Wilson and the stirring events that had transpired during the intervening three years.

The formation was led by Brigadier General Neville and his brigade staff, including Lem Shepherd, all mounted. The troops were formed in ranks 26 men abreast—clad in steel helmets and khaki field uniforms with leggings, field packs, and cartridge belts, and carrying rifles with fixed bayonets. Many had their 2nd Division insignia—a red Indian head (in full headdress of black-tipped white eagle feathers) upon a white star superimposed on a black shield—affixed to their helmets. Sixty wounded Marines brought up the rear of the marchers, transported in ambulances or private cars. About one hundred crippled soldiers from the Army's Walter Reed General Hospital—many of whom served with the Marines in France—were positioned to the left of the reviewing stand that was set up in front of the White House.[3]

Shepherd's service in World War I came to an end. His two years of duty in France with the American Expeditionary Force had been a thrilling experience and changed the pattern of his life. Instead of becoming a civil engineer as he had planned, he became a professional soldier in the United States Marine Corps. Shepherd liked service life and, after discussing it with his regimental commander, decided to remain in the Marine Corps. His father was somewhat disappointed, as he wished him to study medicine and take over his practice. His mother approved of his decision to serve his country, however. An opportunity to go back to France gave him an excuse to postpone the final decision.

Shepherd's valorous service with a frontline combat unit brought him honors: the Army Distinguished Service Cross, the Navy Cross, the Croix de Guerre, and citation in dispatches of the 2nd Division. Of even greater importance, the intensive training and the bitter fighting provided him with a firm elementary grounding in leadership. And it convinced him, beyond question, that the Marine Corps was the life for him.

CHAPTER 11

Mapping Belleau Wood, September 1919–December 1920

Shepherd's friendship with Major Barrett paid dividends when he was asked to return to France to assist Barrett with making a relief map of Belleau Wood. Barrett thought a map of Belleau Wood would be of great historical significance because it was the greatest battle the Marine Corps had ever participated in. He asked Shepherd to accompany him because of his civil engineering degree from VMI and because he had some experience in topographical sketching. Shepherd jumped at the opportunity even though he would only have a weekend to see his parents.

On September 3, 1919, the 11-member France Map Detachment, as it was named (four officers, a warrant officer, four sergeants, and two privates), embarked on the USS *Sol Navis*, a small, slow-moving naval supply ship, for France. Shepherd spent most of his time on the voyage studying for the Marine Corps probationary examination. His two-year probationary period was over, and in order to qualify for a regular commission he had to take the exam. Major Barrett, who had been an instructor in the Marine Corps Schools, volunteered to assist him. The examination covered everything "under the sun … [so] you had to know your books."[1] Shepherd took the examination, which lasted several days, soon after arrival in France and passed with flying colors. His commission as a permanent captain was confirmed by Congress soon after.

The *Sol Navis* docked at Brest, France, on Sunday, September 14, the beginning of a three-month expedition to produce a detailed relief map of Belleau Wood. The scale was one inch on the map to 100 feet on the ground. The scale enabled creation of a detailed and very accurate map of the terrain. Plotting the houses in the villages and numerous barns around each farmhouse took a great deal of time, however, especially the parts of houses that had been struck and damaged by shellfire. The trenches were still there and quite obvious because of the chalky soil. Everywhere there was a trench dug there was a white line. As they were mapping the Belleau Wood area, they found the skeletons of a Marine and a German—their uniforms still on—in a well and other remains in the grass and thickets. The fallen were recovered and buried in the Belleau Wood Cemetery.[2]

After performing an initial survey of the battlefield, Major Barrett divided the detachment into two mapping parties, each with an officer to do the sketching and another on the transit with two enlisted rodmen. Shepherd's team was assigned to the western portion of the battlefield, which included Les Mares farm. Major Barrett rented an office where the enlisted draftsmen transposed the topographical sketching to a master map. Shepherd's draftsmen turned out to be unsatisfactory, so he had to train them on the job, which initially delayed the work of transposing the sketches onto the master map. Les Mares farm was not far from the tree where Shepherd received his first wound. He didn't have any difficulty locating it. He found seven bullet holes in the trunk of the tree, grouped at the height of his head.[3]

At one point during the project, Shepherd thought they were jinxed. First, one of the officers was hospitalized in Paris for two weeks. Then one of Shepherd's rodmen was placed on the sick list. Then he was standing in front of the open fire one evening in his room, after having removed his wet boots, when suddenly the logs shifted, upsetting an open container of boiling water on his feet and ankles. The woolen socks he was wearing absorbed the scalding water. When he removed his socks he found the skin around his ankles badly burned and blistered. He hobbled around in a pair of French peasants' wooden shoes for several days.[4]

Despite illnesses and injuries, the mapping was completed by the middle of December, and on January 1, 1920, the detachment bid goodbye to Belleau Wood and embarked on the USAT *George Washington* for home. To add insult to injury, the voyage to the United States was a rough one.

The ship ran into a powerful storm, and the next several days were among the worst Shepherd had ever spent at sea. The seas were so heavy that they washed away several lifeboats. It was a happy day when he entered New York Harbor and entrained for Quantico.[5]

The detachment spent the next three months completing the relief map. The finished plaster of Paris relief map was approximately 16 feet square and included all of Belleau Wood and an area of equal size to the west which included Hill 142 and Les Mares Farm,[6] and showed every terrain feature in detail—woods, fields, farms, and individual houses. The [map] was greatly admired and subsequently placed in the Smithsonian Institution, where it remained for many years. The commandant assigned a Marine sergeant who had lost his arm at Belleau Wood to duty at the Smithsonian Institution to describe the various phases of the battle to the tourists who visited the building. The map was later stored at the Quantico Marine Base.[7]

Shepherd was not through with relief maps. The Belleau Wood map received such a great deal of positive comments that the commandant directed a second expedition to France to map other battlefields where the Marines had fought—Soissons, Saint-Mihiel, Blanc Mont, and the Meuse–Argonne offensive. Shepherd served as the executive officer of the expedition. He sailed on the USAT *Mercury* on May 20, landing in Saint-Nazaire two weeks later. The expedition consisted of 12 officers and 48 enlisted men, divided into two mapping parties. Shepherd was particularly interested in the Blanc Mont battlefield, where he had received his third wound. He explored the elaborate German machine gun emplacements and dugouts. He was more impressed than ever with how the 4th Brigade ever captured them. He found one machine gun emplacement in particular, close to the spot where his platoon joined up with the French, that was truly a work of defensive art. It was circular in form and constructed of concrete with firing apertures on all sides and sufficient room inside to house an entire platoon. He dreaded to think how many men were lost in capturing it.

The expedition completed its work and, after a final liberty in Paris, left for Antwerp to catch the USAT *Pocahontas* back to the United States. The maps were completed at Quantico similar to the one of Belleau

Wood, and for years they were used by the Marine Corps Schools for historical purposes.

During the second mapping expedition Shepherd was able to visit a number of art galleries and other famous places of interest in Europe that influenced his cultural background and gave him a totally different view of Marine Corps life from what he had led in the combat zone. These experiences strengthened his decision to make the Marine Corps a career. He certainly hadn't counted on a military career.[8]

Lem Shepherd came home from France a proven, highly decorated combat leader, with a U.S. Army Distinguished Service Cross, Navy Cross, Silver Star, and a French Croix de Guerre. He was a charter member of the "Marine Brigade," a clique of young officers linked by personal and professional relationships forged on the battlefields of France who would leave their mark on the Marine Corps in the years to come.

CHAPTER 12

Interwar Years, 1920–1943

Aide-de-Camp

Shepherd returned to the United States in December 1920, and upon returning from a visit with his parents, he found orders to report to the commandant of the Marine Corps, General John A. Lejeune, as aide-de-camp. He never learned who suggested his name for the highly sought-after duty. The experiences thus far in his career strengthened his decision to make the Marine Corps his career, a decision he never regretted.

Shepherd particularly enjoyed the early morning horseback rides. Every morning at seven o'clock he met General Lejeune and Captain John Craige, the senior aide, at "Eighth and Eye (Marine Barracks)" with horses, and the three of them rode through southeast Washington around Hains Point, arriving at Headquarters Marine Corps at exactly nine o'clock. Shepherd by this time had his own horse (an aide could draw a forage allowance), which he boarded at the Washington Riding and Hunt Club near the Q Street Bridge. In the afternoon he took long rides in Rock Creek Park. Less than two months after becoming Lejeune's aide, he was selected to be a White House social aide during President Warren G. Harding's administration.[1]

International Exposition

After two years in Washington, Captain Shepherd was detailed in the summer of 1922 to command the 83d Company, 6th Marines, which was being sent to the International Exposition being held in Rio de Janeiro. The company of specially selected Marines consisted of four platoons, a small headquarters company, the 6th Marines regimental band, and a supply unit and bakery. They wore specially tailored blue uniforms with white trousers. Shepherd set up a model tent camp right in the center of Rio de Janeiro.[2] He was authorized $3,401.44 for equipment and expenses. Every day the company conducted a formal guard mount and parade. On various occasions they marched throughout the city, the exposition grounds, and for various officials who visited there. Shepherd thought it was a great public relations assignment. The company also fielded a baseball team that took on all comers.

Upon the conclusion of the exposition, Shepherd returned to the United States with orders to Norfolk and sea duty as Marine detachment commander aboard the battleship USS *Idaho* (BB-42).[3] It was a very convenient assignment. He was engaged to Virginia Tunstall Driver, whose father, Dr. Wilson Driver, was, like Shepherd's father, a Norfolk physician. Their marriage was on December 30, 1922, in Norfolk's St. Paul's Episcopal Church. After service on the USS *Idaho*, he commanded the East Coast Sea School at Norfolk for two years. The couple's first son, Lemuel C. Shepherd III, best known as "Bo," was born in 1925. Bo enlisted in the Marine Corps from high school in 1943, went to Yale under the V-12 program, and retired as a colonel in 1973. A second son, Wilson E. D. Shepherd, was born in Shanghai in 1928 and soon gained the nickname "DeeDee," derived from the Chinese words for "little brother." Wilson also attended VMI and served in the Marine Corps.[4]

Foreign Service: China

While Shepherd was at Sea School, Marines were deployed to Nicaragua. The commander, Brigadier General Logan Feland, tried to get Shepherd assigned to his staff. Unfortunately, he was unable to get relieved from the school, much to his disappointment. His chance for overseas deployment came in the spring of 1927, when the 3d Brigade was sent to China to protect Americans citizens. Captain Shepherd was so insistent that he be allowed to join the brigade that he received a letter of reprimand, but in the end he got his wish: orders to China. After brief service in North China with the 15th Marines, a temporary regiment, he was assigned to the 4th Marines in Shanghai's International Settlement, where he served as regimental adjutant, for two years. When the situation in China calmed down, Shepherd was allowed to bring his wife over, at his own expense.

The International Settlement had a number of foreign garrisons. Among them were the British troops, which deeply impressed Shepherd with their smartness and military bearing. He especially enjoyed the exchange of mess nights or dining-in with the British. As regimental adjutant he was responsible for the conduct of the 4th Marines' parades. The 1st Battalion of the Green Howards, a Yorkshire regiment, had a fine fife and drum corps that Shepherd set out to emulate. The president of the Shanghai Municipal Council was a Mr. Fessenden who saw to it that the 4th Marines were provided with the necessary instruments, and the new musical assemblage was named the Fessenden Fifes. Marine buglers, or "field music" as they were then called, were taught to play the fifes and drums by the Green Howards drum major. Once a week the 4th Marines would parade through the streets of Shanghai to the beat of the music of the Fessenden Fifes. When the Green Howards left Shanghai, the Fessenden Fifes marched them down to the Bund and onto their ship.[5]

Shepherd returned from China in April 1929 to attend the nine-months-long Field Officers Course at Marine Corps Schools, Quantico. While he was there his daughter, Virginia Cartwright, was born, nicknamed "Siddie" from her young brothers' efforts to say "sister." In 1951 she would marry the general's former aide, Captain (now Colonel, Retired) James B. Ord Jr.

Garde d'Haiti

In the 1930s, the Marine Corps established a constabulary in Haiti. The newly assigned Brigadier General R. P. Williams, commanding officer, 2nd Regiment, Garde d'Haiti, requested Captain Shepherd's service in the Garde d'Haiti. At the time, Shepherd had been a company grade officer for 17 years.

Shepherd was temporarily promoted to major, a rank he held for the entire tour, and given command of the Caserne Dartiguenave (the main barracks for troops) in Port-au-Prince. It was a tense time, Haitian elements were near revolution, and there was political unrest throughout the country. After two years at the Caserne, he was assigned as police chief of the city from June 1932 to June 1933. "As Chief of Police, part of the assignment was to keep the American minister advised on the political situation. Shepherd proved his skill in handling uprisings. Time after time, as mob reactions were kindled by disgruntled politicians, under his direction potentially dangerous disorders were quickly and firmly smothered by opportune action."[6]

The last year of his assignment, Shepherd commanded the department of Port-au-Prince, which covered the entire center of the country. Not one to sit behind a desk, Shepherd renewed his love of horses by playing polo, and going riding once every three months for 10 days at a time, checking on the various Haitian guard stations along the Santo Domingo border. Like many officers who served in Haiti, Shepherd picked up the habit of carrying a Haitian walking stick, called a coco macaque, whenever he was in the field. Later in his career, photos showed him carrying the stick. Shepherd found the four years in Haiti interesting and a great experience for a young officer. He gained valuable experience that would stand him in good stead in the years to come.

Marine Barracks, Washington

Following the withdrawal of the Marines from Haiti in 1934, Major Shepherd was detailed as executive officer and registrar of the Marine Corps Institute at the Marine Barracks, Washington, D.C. The assignment had been requested by the new major general commandant, John Russell, who had known Shepherd in Haiti. For several months, he was the acting commanding officer of the barracks, normally a colonel's billet. It was with considerable pride that he was able to reflect on events that had transpired since that fateful day of April 11, 1917, and of his progress up the ladder of success in the profession he had selected as his life's work.[7]

He was ordered by Major General Russell to smarten up the barracks into a more military organization. Shepherd—who believed in the importance of Marine Corps history, particularly the snap and precision of marching and drill—began the assignment by ordering a parade and guard mount every morning and a full-dress afternoon parade once a week for guests, which continues to this very day with a Friday evening parade. He also organized a drum and bugle corps, now known as "The Commandant's Own," along the model of the Shanghai Fessenden Fifes. At the request of the assistant commandant, he prepared a manual for drummers and trumpeters—"Manual for Drummers, Buglers and Fifers"—even though he did not have a musical background. The job was harder than he thought. He had to get permission from Mrs. Sousa, wife of John Philip Sousa, composer of American military marches, to use parts of her husband's marches and other copyrights before publication. In addition to these duties, Shepherd was assigned to organize a detachment of Marines to guard President Roosevelt when he visited Warm Springs, Georgia—the "Little White House"—every fall. He took the assignment very seriously and heaved a great sigh of relief when the president returned to Washington.

Wartime Unit

Now a lieutenant colonel, promoted in 1936, Shepherd wanted to improve himself professionally, and, after two years at the barracks, he asked the commandant to send him to the Naval War College in Newport, Rhode Island. Upon finishing the course in June 1937, he was given command of the 2d Battalion, 5th Marines, his old wartime outfit, stationed at Quantico, Virginia. The battalion was part of the newly formed Fleet Marine Force, Atlantic, which was being extensively employed in the development of amphibious tactics and techniques. Shepherd's battalion was called up to test several of the new tactical developments, one of them being whether or not a night landing from boats could be made on a hostile beach. There were strong arguments that it couldn't be done. Shepherd was confident he could do it and proved he was right by putting his battalion ashore at Ponce, Puerto Rico, at night within a hundred yards of the objective. The aggressors were caught completely by surprise and taken prisoner. The Army officer in charge of the aggressor was Walter Short, the same officer who was surprised by the Japanese at Pearl Harbor on December 7, 1941.[8]

As a battalion commander, Shepherd served as a member of the Equipment Board and headed the motor transport and tank committee. During that time, he got involved in the controversy involving the amphibious tractor: Was it a boat or was it a motor vehicle? The members kept passing the question off from one to another until a decision was reached by Colonel Merritt Edson at Guadalcanal, who decided that it was an assault vehicle. Another issue involving Shepherd was the weight of the tank. Initially, he found that a tank was limited to five tons because it was thought the Navy's boom could only lift five tons. Shepherd found that this was not true: the Navy booms could lift 15 tons. He recommended that the Marine Corps purchase the U.S. Army's excellent light tank because they were within the 15-ton limitation.

CHAPTER 13

Striking Ninth, 1943–1944

In 1939 Shepherd was transferred to the Marine Corps Schools at Quantico and assigned as director of the Correspondence School, where he rewrote the text on combat intelligence and was the officer in charge of the candidates' class. It was during this period that the amphibious doctrine was originated, evolved, and tested. A year later, he was promoted to colonel and became assistant commandant of the Marine Corps Schools. By the time World War II began, the Corps was preparing for war. Shepherd was involved in making extensive studies of techniques and tactics that were being used and how they could be employed by the Marine Corps. He thought it was a very interesting type of assignment and one from which he learned a great deal. The day after the Japanese bombed Pearl Harbor, he received orders to send a number of officers to strategic points along the East Coast of the North American continent and islands to check whether the German submarines had landed agents. Shepherd was also assigned as an observer and staff member on the Army maneuvers that were taking place at Camden, South Carolina, and Manassas, Virginia. He learned a great deal, even though they were "canned" exercises. The troops had wooden rifles and stovepipes instead of regular weapons and mortars.[1]

On March 16, 1943, four months after Pearl Harbor, Shepherd was selected to organize and train the newly reactivated 9th Marine Regiment (Striking Ninth), which had been disbanded after World War I. The regiment was formed at Camp Elliott, San Diego, as part of the 2nd Marine Division. When Shepherd took command, there was only one battalion, but it was subsequently brought up to strength by a cadre of officers and men from the 2nd Marines, 3d Battalion, 6th Marines, and reserves and recruits from the Marine Corps Recruit Depot in San Diego. Shepherd was known as a positive leader, one who encouraged the best in his men. He had a tough side, however, and could "kick your ass if he felt you deserved it," according to one of his officers. A story circulated that one of his officers transferred to the Raiders, which infuriated Shepherd. The transfer came in while he was in the field 10 miles from camp. The officer made the mistake of asking Shepherd for transfer back to camp, but Shepherd refused to provide transportation and the officer picked up his gear and walked.[2]

Shepherd revamped training. He stopped all battalion and company training and instead emphasized individual and small-unit training for the purposes of discipline, morale, and physical conditioning. Following the accomplishment of these objectives, the emphasis was placed on more advanced tactical instruction. The entire program worked toward welding the companies and battalions into a hard-striking, well-trained fighting team. Regimental schools were established to prepare NCOs and privates as instructors in the various units. Shepherd also held semiweekly officers' schools for junior officers. Schools were also established for bayonet training, hand grenades, rifles, machine guns and mortars, rubber boats and commando-raider tactics. Emphasis was placed on physical conditioning, map reading, scouting, and observing.[3]

During May and June, amphibious training was conducted in the San Diego–La Jolla area. Training was interrupted when the regiment sent a battalion to the East Coast to form the nucleus of a new regiment. Shepherd was also ordered to furnish a large number of men to the newly formed 22nd and 23d Marines. It wasn't until August that replacements brought the 9th back to full strength. On September 8 the regiment was assigned to the newly formed 3d Marine Division. In the later part of October, the regiment was reinforced and organized into three battalion landing teams.

On January 24, 1943, the regiment sailed for Auckland, New Zealand, aboard the USS *Mt. Vernon*. Shepherd was billeted on the same ship as the division commander, Major General Charles Barnett, and his chief of staff, Colonel Alfred Noble. With the 1st Marine Division's trouble on Guadalcanal with moving supplies from ship to shore fresh in their minds, the three spent the entire voyage working on a standard operating procedure (SOP) for unloading supplies during an amphibious operation. Under General Barnett's direction, Shepherd and Noble produced an SOP for unloading supplies that was used throughout the Marine Corps during World War II and formed the basis for present-day doctrine. The SOP paid dividends when the regiment later moved to Guadalcanal; it completed unloading its supplies and equipment within six hours. When Japanese planes bombed the beach, little or no damage was done to its supply dumps.[4]

Current design of the 9th Marine Regiment based on the earlier design. (Public Domain)

Upon arrival in Auckland on February 5, the regiment disembarked two days later and was billeted in several dispersed sites because of a lack of space large enough to accommodate the entire regiment. The camps were widely separated, a distance of over 20 miles from the furthest battalion to regimental headquarters, which was located at a racetrack near Pukekohe, a town 30 miles south of Auckland. Shepherd immediately ordered the battalions to conduct intensive training, within the limitations imposed by geography. Training included weapons familiarization; techniques of jungle warfare; scouting and patrolling; squad, platoon, and company exercises; and conditioning hikes of up to 60 miles. In the early morning hours of June 29, the regiment boarded five transports and sailed for Guadalcanal.[5]

After an uneventful voyage, the regiment arrived at Guadalcanal on July 6 and established camp in a large coconut grove three miles from Tetere Village and 12 miles southeast of Henderson Field. While the main

Japanese force had been defeated, there were still Japanese holdouts on the island, which gave the Marines an incentive for active patrolling … and the patrols occasionally found one. On July 19, Major General Barrett promoted Shepherd to brigadier general and announced that he was being assigned as the assistant division commander of the 1st Marine Division, then under the command of Major General William H. Rupertus. Shepherd was told that he would take over the division after serving a period of indoctrination. While he was happy to be promoted, he was disappointed to leave the regiment before taking it into combat.[6]

CHAPTER 14

The Green Inferno, January 1944

For the New Britain operation, Brigadier General Shepherd was initially assigned command of Combat Team A, a semi-independent command, built around the 7th Marines and the 3d Battalion, 5th Marines. Initially Shepherd experienced some difficulty in getting a few of his subordinates to follow his orders wholeheartedly. He wasn't a member of the close-knit Guadalcanal clique. Shepherd felt that after Cape Gloucester (codenamed Operation *Backhander*, was fought between December 26, 1943, and January 16, 1944) he had convinced his subordinates that his ideas were sound.[1]

Shepherd prepared plans for a landing on the south shore of New Britain at Linderhafen Plantation and to seize the nearby Japanese base at Gasmata. The landing was called off at the last minute. Instead, he went in with the division on December 26 to Cape Gloucester. He was given three missions: to defend the landing area, to expand the perimeter to the southwest, and to clear the enemy from the Borgen Bay area. The last mission turned out to be the major battle on New Britain.[2]

Shepherd compared the fight through the near impenetrable jungle around Borgen Bay to Grant's fight through the Wilderness because his command had to fight through an unknown territory, dense jungle, swamps, and high hills. The weather added to the difficulty. The day after Shepherd landed, a 21-day typhoon swept through with 20 or 30 inches of rain a day, leaving everything in a quagmire. The troops were miserable, and the typhoon delayed landing equipment and supplies. Cape Gloucester was described as "wet and less wet." The rainforest produced

Ghost Trail. Drawing; charcoal and pastel on paper; by Kerr Eby; 1944. (Naval History and Heritage Command)

giant trees towering up to two hundred feet into the sky above dense undergrowth lashed together by savage vines as thick as a man's arm and many times as tough, interspersed with occasional patches of kunai grass, sometimes higher than a man's head, and hip-deep swamps.[3]

The division's report noted, "Water backed up in the swamps in rear of the shoreline, making them impassible for wheeled and tracked vehicles. The many streams which emptied into the sea in the beachhead area became raging torrents. Some even changed their course. Troops were soaked to the skin and their clothes never dried out during the entire campaign."

On New Year's Day, 1944, Shepherd launched his force, supported by the 1st and 4th Battalions, 11th Marines (artillery), to attack toward Borgen Bay. At the time, he did not know the Japanese were withdrawing from Cape Gloucester and the other side of the island through Aogiri Ridge, the junction of two major trails, which the Japanese used extensively. A captured Japanese document found on a dead warrant officer stated that Aogiri Ridge was to be held at all costs. Shepherd did not have any maps of the island and did not know where the ridge was. The name meant nothing to him.

Suicide Creek

On the morning of January 2, the scouts from 3/7 and 3/5 reached a broad, innocent-looking stream that ran between high banks, twenty to thirty feet across with brackish water from knee to waist deep. The scouts waded into the water and started across in the face of scattered sniper fire. After gaining the opposite bank, they motioned the rest of the platoon to cross. Suddenly the scouts saw several Japanese, who opened fire from several expertly camouflaged machine-gun positions dug in along the stream bank.[4]

Machine-gun fire swept the Marines from every direction. The platoon was pinned down with its back to the water. All they could do was hug the ground as bullets cut the brush above their heads. The men tried all day to get across the creek, but in the end, they had to withdraw to a ridge on the American side and dig in for the night. At dawn the next morning, the Japanese launched a devastating mortar attack. All the next day small units tried to push across the creek at different points, trying to find a soft spot in the Japanese defenses.

Late in the afternoon on January 3 an unarmored bulldozer and three Sherman tanks worked their way over a rough-hewn track to a position in the center of the Japanese defenses. The bulldozer operator was shot and evacuated, but two other volunteers crawled forward and dug a useable ramp for tanks to cross the stream.

The final assault began the next morning after a 15-minute artillery preparation. The three Shermans eased their way down the earthen ramp and through the shallow water, up the far bank, and right into the heart of the enemy position. Using tank-infantry tactics, the dug-in Japanese defenses were expertly destroyed by point-blank cannon fire or crushed under tank treads. The battle of Suicide Creek was over, but the cost had been heavy: 36 Marines had died, 218 were wounded, and five were missing in action.

The advance continued until it reached Aogiri Ridge. Shepherd came up to the front lines to personally observe the attack on the ridge. He worked his way forward to where Lieutenant Colonel Lew "Silent Lew" Walt, commanding officer, 3d Battalion, 5th Marines, was directing the attack. The two were lying on the ground close to the roots of a banyan tree observing a firefight about 40 yards away when Walt suddenly lurched against Shepherd. He had been hit in the pack on his back, and the force of the blow knocked him against Shepherd.[5]

In the initial attack on the ridge, Walt's battalion was pinned down. He ordered a 37-mm gun forward to fire canister at the ridge. The gunner fired several rounds, but the gun became a target of the Japanese fire, which killed and wounded the crew. Walt yelled for replacements, but when no one responded, Walt and his runner started pushing the gun up the steep slope. Seeing the battalion commander pushing the gun, several Marines jumped up to help. They finally reached the top and dug in for the night. Shepherd thought Walt's bravery on Aogiri Ridge was the greatest demonstration of leadership he had ever witnessed. He thought Walt had demonstrated how the will of a commander can influence an entire battle. In honor of Walt's bravery and leadership, Shepherd had Aogiri Ridge renamed Walt's Ridge.

That night the Japanese made five all-out attacks against the ridge, but they were never able to drive the Marines off the hill. In one attack, a Japanese officer died within three paces of Walt's foxhole, where he crouched, .45 in hand. The next morning Shepherd inspected the battlefield and found the bodies of Marines and Japanese scattered over the hilltop, some as close as six feet from one another. Shepherd thought the battle for the ridge was the critical battle of the Cape Gloucester campaign. The ridge protected a major trail junction through which all Japanese troops and supplies in the mountains and back of Cape Gloucester had to feed. With this important junction in hand, the brigade was able to kill or capture the Japanese withdrawing down the coast toward Rabaul.

Shepherd ordered 3d Battalion, 7th Marines under Lieutenant Colonel Henry W. Buse, supported by tanks and half-tracks, to move against Hill 660. It was the last piece of high ground in enemy hands that could interfere with operations on the beaches. The Japanese occupying the hill were estimated to be one reinforced company. At 9:30 a.m. on January 13, after heavy preparation by artillery, mortars, and air, 3d Battalion began its approach through a deep gulch, both slopes cluttered with jungle undergrowth and strewn with boulders. The slope was so steep that men sometimes had to crawl upward on all fours under Japanese fire.

The battalion finally reached the top just as night fell on January 14. The capture of Hill 660 marked the last of the heavy fighting. From then until the island was secured, the fight became one of Japanese flight and pursuit by strong Marine combat patrols. Shepherd also used a company in boats to intercept the coastal trail and cut off the Japanese retreat. Tactically, his plan to defeat the Japanese was to push them from behind and jump ahead by sea to block their retreat.

Although Shepherd was awarded a Legion of Merit for exceptionally meritorious service in command of operations in the Borgen Bay area, he believed the Cape Gloucester campaign didn't get the recognition it deserved, partly because Tarawa followed shortly afterward and overshadowed it.

The meetings Shepherd had with General MacArthur during Cape Gloucester would pay off in the future during the Korean War, when MacArthur asked for the 1st Marine Division.

CHAPTER 15

1st Marine Brigade, Operation *Stevedore*, July–August 1944

Liberation of Guam

While still on New Britain, Shepherd received orders on Easter morning, 1944, to return to Pearl Harbor to command the 1st Provisional Marine Brigade. At the time, he had been told he was going to take over the 1st Marine Division from Rupertus, and he was very much looking forward to the assignment, so it was with great regret that he left Cape Gloucester to fly to Pearl Harbor. Upon arrival in Hawaii, he was briefed and formally assigned the command of the 1st Provisional Marine Brigade by the acerbic "Howlin' Mad" Smith, commanding general of the Fleet Marine Force. While there, Shepherd was able to observe one component of his brigade, the veteran 22nd Marines, which was refitting and training on the Big Island after returning from seizing the island of Kwajalein in the Central Pacific. Shepherd spent a few days in Honolulu before sailing for Guadalcanal with the regiment, where they would link up with the 4th Marines.[1]

The 4th Marine Regiment, commanded by Lieutenant Colonel Alan Shapley, was rather unique. The men of the original regiment were languishing in Japanese prison camps, after being captured when the Philippines fell in April 1942. The "new" regiment was reconstituted by combining the Raider battalions after General Alexander Vandegrift decided that they "were divisive to the Corps because they fostered the concept of elitism." Initially the Raiders were unhappy that their organization was broken up. Shepherd was concerned that they thought of themselves as individuals, but they turned into one of the best units in the brigade under the strong leadership of Shapley. The 22nd Marines also had a strong commander and were used to operating independently. The two regimental commanders were jealous of their prerogatives and loath to employ their troops and supporting elements in unified brigade action. An example often quoted by Shepherd was one regimental commander protesting that he wanted only his own artillery battalion to support him and did not desire the combined fires of the brigade artillery group to support the attack of his regiment, which happened to be the main effort of that day. The same hesitancy applied to the use of tanks under brigade control. Shepherd's focus was to mold two reinforced infantry regiments into a unified brigade fighting force.[2]

Some years after the war, one of Shepherd's regimental commanders remarked to him that when he subsequently commanded a division, he learned to appreciate the difficulties with which Shepherd had confronted on taking command of the brigade: "He had admired the patience I had exercised with him during the above period and regretted the headaches he had caused me at the time."[3]

The brigade was assigned to the extreme western end of Guadalcanal 10 miles from Henderson Field, at a place called Tetere, to train for the Guam operation. Shepherd considered the area to be excellent for training, as there were three separate cul-de-sacs where it could conduct three battalion maneuvers and firing exercises at the same time.

The recapture of Guam had been a long-standing student exercise at the various military schools. In fact, Shepherd had prepared a detailed plan for the capture of the island at the Naval War College, so he knew it pretty well. His study noted that the landing beaches were limited because of the fringing reefs. The development of the amphibious tractor changed the entire picture, however, opening up several additional landing beaches. Unfortunately, on the Guam landing, there were only enough amphibious tractors to boat the first few waves, and after being savaged by Japanese anti-boat guns there were even fewer.[4]

Serious planning for Operation *Stevedore* began on April 27 with the receipt of a staff memorandum from Admiral Richmond Kelly Turner. Shepherd tried to acquire additional junior officers to fill essential jobs in the Brigade Headquarter Company and his staff. Requests to Major General Allen H. Turnage, commanding general, 3d Marine Division, were stonewalled—"No officers available"—so Shepherd and his chief of staff had to write many of the operation orders themselves, much to his chagrin. Shepherd claimed that the 3d Marine Division had an excess of officers. He extracted some revenge later when the brigade beat the division to an assigned linkup point. He wrote a message to Turnage noting that the brigade was at the linkup, where was he?[5]

Despite being short-staffed, the brigade completed Operation Plan Number 1 on May 22. The plan provided for a landing by two regimental combat teams (RCTs) abreast to seize a beachhead between the town of Agat and Bangi Point, and then a drive north and west to capture Orote Peninsula. The two regimental beaches were separated by stubbornly defended Ga'an Point: The 4th Marines, commanded by Lieutenant Colonel Alan Shapley, would land over White Beaches 1 and 2 to seize Alifan Ridge, the high ground to their front. The 22d Marines, commanded by Colonel Merlin F. Schneider, would land over Yellow Beaches 1 and 2, then pivot north to meet 3d Marine Division elements at the base of Orote Peninsula. U.S. Army's 305th RCT was designated the brigade's floating reserve. Opposing the American force were two battalions of the 38th Infantry, reinforced by a company of the 9th Tank Regiment on the landing beaches and the 54th Naval Guard Force dug in on the Orote Peninsula.[6]

W-day (D-day) was scheduled for 8:30 a.m. on July 21. The plan for the landing on Guam called for a simultaneous landing of the 20,000-man 3d Marine Division's three regiments abreast on Asan Point, to capture the high ground immediately inland. Shepherd's 9,000-man First Provisional Marine Brigade landed south about five miles away in the vicinity of Agat and then drove north to isolate the Orote Peninsula. The 305th Regimental Combat Team of the 77th Division was initially attached to the brigade. Shepherd envisioned that the amphibious tractors transporting the initial waves would go inland five hundred yards before disembarking the troops. The Army's 77th Infantry Division, commanded by Major General Andrew D. Bruce, would follow up the brigade's initial landings and fight alongside the Marines in the drive north. The Corps artillery under Brigadier General Pedro A. del Valle supported the three infantry units.[7]

Captured enemy documents indicated that the Japanese 29th Division and various naval base and defense troops, some 19 thousand men, garrisoned the island. They were well supplied with coast artillery, antiaircraft guns, and field artillery, which were heavily camouflaged and cleverly emplaced to disrupt and destroy an enemy landing. The western beaches were studded with mines and anti-boat obstacles. Machine guns and mortars were sited to provide covering fire. The Japanese commander knew the Americans were coming and pushed his men to prepare. He thought they had an excellent opportunity to annihilate them on the beaches but didn't take into account naval gunfire support of Rear Admiral R. L. "Close In" Connelly, who told Shepherd that he would run his flagship onto the beach if necessary. Shepherd was not impressed with the naval bombardment, however. When he got ashore, he did not find that much damage, even though the ships had shelled the beaches for days.

Blood on the Reef

Shepherd watched the assault waves in amphibious tractors (amtracs) crawl out of the sea onto the wide fringing reef that fronted the brigade's landing beaches. The Japanese beach defenses were well organized. Concrete pillboxes, machine gun emplacements, and an elaborate trench system protected the enemy from the initial naval gunfire, and when the landing craft came within range, the defenders opened up with everything they had. Machine gun fire from emplacements along the beach caused many casualties. Anti-boat gunfire was heavy and accurate, knocking out a dozen amtracs and leaving them burning in the water. One exploded, sending debris flying through the air. The sand-covered, concrete-faced blockhouse with a four-foot-thick roof was built into the nose of Ga'an Point and could enfilade the beaches. It held 75-mm and 37-mm guns, which raked Yellow Beach 2, a 300-yard strip of sand, knocking out two dozen amtracs and killing 75 men of the 22nd Marines, before Marine tanks knocked them out with their main guns.[8]

Midmorning, Shepherd, with his forward command group, disembarked from the transport and started for the beach. The first assault wave had barely cleared the first low ridge when Shepherd's amtrac lumbered out of the water. He and his small forward CP (command post) group climbed over the gunwales, dropped to the beach, and scrambled for cover. They set up in a coconut grove about two hundred yards southeast of Ga'an Point, where moments earlier, tanks had knocked out the particularly troublesome emplacement. By early afternoon, Shepherd's command post was up and running, and he assumed control of all troops in his zone of action. He pushed his commanders to get off the beach.

The 4th Marines moved forward across open fields to the Alifan massif. By late afternoon, the regiment dug in for the night on the western slopes of Mount Alifan's high ground, a beachhead some 45 hundred yards wide and two thousand yards deep.[9] The 22nd Marines seized the village of Agat and the high ground to the north, tying in with the 4th Marines on its right flank. Shepherd issued orders for night defense and a warning to pay particular attention to organizing in depth and to maintain local reserves as a counterattack force. Shortly before midnight Japanese began probing all along the brigade front. At about 2:30 a.m. four Japanese tanks leading truck-mounted guns and infantry attempted to smash through a roadblock on Harmon Road and break through to Agat. Another enemy attack hit the left center of the 22nd Marines front. All the attacks were repulsed with heavy Japanese losses; the 1st and 2nd Battalions of the 38th Infantry were destroyed as a fighting force. After four days of heavy combat, the brigade had cut off the Orote Peninsula, but it had not been without cost; one thousand Marine were casualties, of whom 188 were killed in action.

Orote Peninsula

By July 25, the brigade stretched across the neck of the heavily defended, eight-square-mile Orote Peninsula, which contained the airfield and the old Marine barracks—4th Marines on the left, its objectives the rifle range and airfield; 22nd Marines on the right, its objectives the old Marine barracks and the town of Sumay. Shepherd gave them one day off to get into position. On July 26 they were ready for the assault. Facing them were more than 25 hundred members of the Special Naval Landing Force, sometimes referred to as Japanese Marines from the 54th Naval Guard Force (*Keibitai*), remnants of the 38th Infantry Regiment, and various support units, under the command of Air Group Commander Asaichi Tamai. The attack was a tough one; the Japanese had constructed an elaborate interlocking system of pillboxes, strongpoints, and trenches.[10]

Promptly at seven o'clock, Shepherd ordered the brigade to attack. The two regiments jumped off, after a heavy 15-minute artillery preparation—one artillery battalion fired a thousand rounds in support. The regiments had to attack on a narrow front because of mangrove swamps that channelized them.

The 4th Marines ran into a buzz saw when it ran into one of the strongest defensive lines on the peninsula. General Shepherd just happened to be on one of his daily frontline visits and observed the action. He immediately obtained a platoon of light tanks and a platoon of tank destroyers from the 77th Division to support the attack. In a fine display of tank-infantry coordination, the strongpoints were destroyed and the surviving Japanese put to rout. Marines counted approximately 250 pillboxes and emplacements in the general area of the attack.[11]

The 22nd Regiment pressed forward and by noon reached the blackened rubble and skeleton buildings of the former Marine barracks. Only a cigar box containing prewar post exchange papers and receipts, a bronze plaque, and a star-covered pillow that a Japanese had made from the blue field of an American flag gave evidence of the former Marine garrison. That afternoon, with artillery booming in the background and the occasional snap of small arms fire, a group of high-ranking Marine officers, including Generals Geiger, Shepherd, and Howlin' Smith, gathered on the grounds and snapped to attention as a bugler sounded "To the Colors" on a captured Japanese bugle. A United States flag was run up the same flagpole that had been there before the war for the first time since the dismal December day in 1941 when the Japanese had invaded in overwhelming force. The brigade continued up the northern tip of the island, overcoming Japanese resistance, including a last ditch all-out banzai attack, before it was declared secure on August 10, 1944.

General Howlin' Smith summed up the brigade's achievement: "The capture of the Orote Peninsula was, in some respects, the outstanding accomplishment of the Guam campaign." It was not without cost, however: 115 Marines of the brigade were killed in action, and more than seven hundred were wounded. Japanese losses on the peninsula totaled 25 hundred.[12]

Final Drive

The 4th Marines, after only three days in reserve, was again thrown into the line on the Corps' left flank in what was to be the final drive of the Guam campaign. The 3d and 77th Divisions had, by August 6, broken through the outer lines of defense and bottled up the remaining organized Japanese units on and near Mount Santa Rosa. In a drive to smash this final bastion and to sweep up stragglers and isolated pockets of resistance, Geiger planned to use all his major combat units.

The 1st Provisional Brigade attacked north along the west coast. Shepherd received the Corps operations plan on August 5 ordering the brigade to pass through the 3d Marines (1st Marine Division) and attack north along the west coast of Guam, then clear the enemy from the northern part of the island by small unit patrols. As the 3d Division's right flank unit, the 9th Marines, led by his old friend Colonel Edward A. "Eddy" Craig, was tasked to make contact with the 1st Marine Brigade. The brigade was working its way north on the Orote Peninsula. Craig was anticipating making contact on July 26. "I was in great hopes of pushing ahead and making contact with the Brigade by nightfall." Instead, he received an order from the assistant division commander to fall back. "I tried to argue against such a move ... however I didn't get very far." Instead, he sent a patrol to make contact. "I was most happy when at 2000 that night the patrol returned with a personal message from General Shepherd." The two finally made contact a few days later. "It was evening when General Shepherd ... came to visit me. He had just arrived when a number of artillery shells started to land in the very near vicinity of my CP. We both ducked behind a cement wall and continued our conversation while sitting on the ground, just two old friends quietly reminiscing in the midst of a shelling!"[13]

The brigade attacked on schedule with two battalions abreast and by midmorning on August 7 had reached its initial objective and continued the attack the next morning against scattered resistance. By 6:00 p.m. on August 9, Shepherd declared that all organized resistance in the brigade's sector had ceased. The next day, the island was declared secure. Guam was the first American territory to be recaptured from Japan.

CHAPTER 16

6th Marine Division, Operation *Iceberg*, 1 April–21 June 1945

The Assault and Capture of Okinawa

After Guam, the brigade returned to Tassafaronga Point on the north coast of Guadalcanal for rehabilitation and to prepare for the assault of Okinawa, Operation *Iceberg*, which Shepherd characterized as a campaign, lasting 89 days.

Major General Lemuel C. Shepherd Jr., USMC, 1945. (Preston Library, Virginia Military Institute)

Major General Lemuel C. Shepherd Jr. consults a map of the Okinawan terrain. (NARA)

Shepherd was promoted to major general, and the brigade, with the addition of the 29th Marines (reinforced) and several other division units, became the 6th Marine Division, with three full infantry regiments and the 15th Artillery Regiment. The division was formed overseas and subsequently disbanded overseas. It never did duty in the United States. He chose Lieutenant Colonel Victor H. Krulak (later lieutenant general) to be his operations officer or G-3, the beginning of a long association.

The three years Shepherd spent studying and teaching tactics at the Marine Corps Schools gave him a leg up when he started a training program that went through squad, platoon, company, battalion, and regimental exercises. The training concentrated on every phase of military operations, all types of warfare, including tank-infantry doctrine, which was best demonstrated in the fighting on Okinawa. In the rapid drive north to the decisive and successful battle for the Motobu Peninsula, the 6th Division Marines rode the tanks that later provided separate fire support in the heavy fighting to rid northern Okinawa of Japanese. In the southern portion of the island, both on level ground and in the cave-studded draws, the tank-infantry team reached a climax, functioning as a major direct fire weapon. By the time the 6th Division shipped out for Okinawa, Shepherd thought it was the best trained organization in the Marine Corps.

The Okinawa invasion force was huge. Its sheer size dwarfed any previous amphibious operation in the Pacific. It was also the largest combined land, sea, and air battle of World War II. The assault forces, designated the Tenth Army and commanded by

General Simon B. Buckner (right) with Major General Lemuel C. Shepherd Jr. (left, with walking stick). (U.S. Government)

Lieutenant General Simon Bolivar Buckner Jr., U.S. Army, consisted of two corps, one army (XXIV Corps, Major General John R. Hodge) and one Marine (III Amphibious Corps, Lieutenant General Roy Geiger), a total of 180 thousand combat troops. The III Amphibious Corps, almost 90 thousand Marines including the 1st, 2nd, and 6th Marine Divisions, embarked on 175 troop and cargo carrying vessels, loaded from nine widely separated embarkation sites.

Fifteen hundred ships supported the operation, everything from battleships and aircraft carriers to specialized landing craft. Facing the Expeditionary Force were 100 thousand diehard Japanese of the Thirty-Second Army, under Lieutenant General Mitsuru Ushijima, with orders to fight to the last man, including a new weapon, suicide pilots of the Japanese navy's Special Attack Corps—Kamikaze (Divine Wind) Corps. The battle lasted from April 1 until June 21, 1945.

Four divisions landed abreast across the Hagushi beaches in the middle of the island on D-day, April 1 (Easter Sunday). Shepherd considered himself a good Christian and believed that the landing on Easter Sunday was a moral crusade, equivalent to fighting against the infidels. The day dawned bright and clear. The temperature was a comfortable 75 degrees. Seas were calm, and a light offshore breeze kept the men in the landing craft from seeing the beaches, shrouded in the smoke and dust from naval gunfire.[1]

Dawn was just breaking when the bombardment started. The whole outline of the island disappeared under the cloud of dust, smoke, and explosives. When the cloud lifted, the planes came over to bomb and strafe, and then the rocket-bearing LCIs rushed in. Finally, armored LVTs swam in leading the first waves of troop-carrying LVTs.[2]

The 6th Marine Division landed on the left flank of the landing beach with two regiments. The 22nd and 4th landed over Green 1 and 2 and Red Beaches 1, 2, and 3, respectively, while the 29th Regiment served as the Corps reserve until 2:45 p.m., when it landed, minus 1/29, over Green 2 and established a reserve position.

Shepherd's initial mission was to capture Yontan airfield while protecting the northern flank of the Tenth Army.

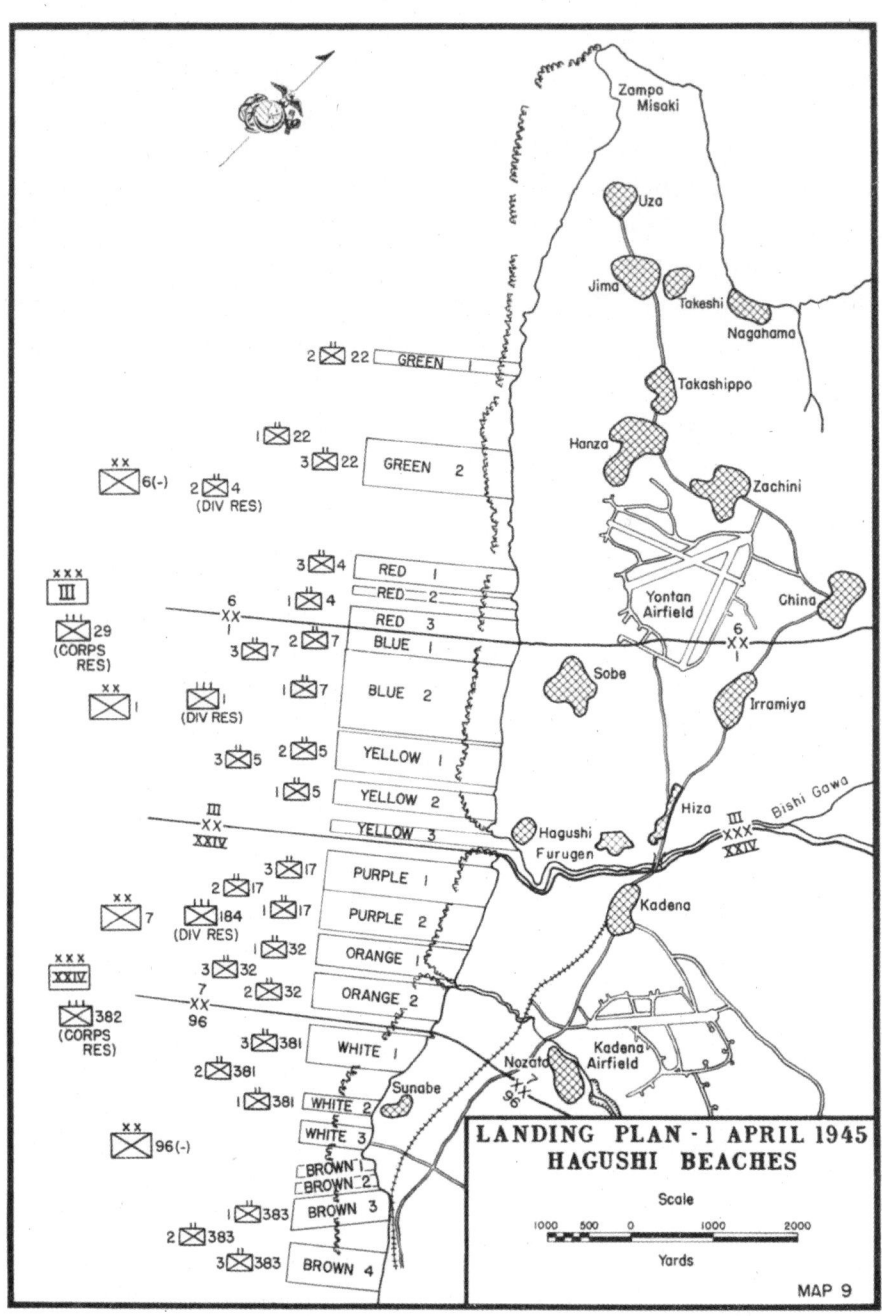

Marine Corps map showing the landing plans for the Hagushi beaches on Okinawa, April 1, 1945. (U.S. Marine Corps)

Shepherd's men poured out of the landing craft expecting to be met by murderous Japanese fire, but only minor resistance was encountered and consisted of mainly isolated pockets built around light machine guns in cave emplacements. Amazingly, the men could walk upright across the beach. The

Imperial Japanese battle flag.

Japanese, in accordance with their defense plan, refrained from firing artillery on the American beachhead and from responding to reconnaissance activities.

The 6th Division seized its first objective, Yontan airfield, by noon on D-day against light to moderate resistance. Shepherd had expected that its capture would take a week or 10 days of heavy fighting. It happened so quickly that a Japanese plane circled the field a couple of times and then landed. The pilot got out carrying a small briefcase and started walking toward the tower when he was taken under fire and killed! It was reported that a veteran sergeant looked at the corpse and said, "There's always some poor SOB that doesn't get the word."[3]

By the end of the first day, Shepherd had landed the division and Corps reserve (2/4 and 1/29) and was in position to continue the attack.

Japanese Battle Slogan

The Japanese posted the Battle Slogan in bunkers as a reminder to the troops to not to "sell" their lives before killing ten of the enemy or destroying one tank.

> One Plane for One Warship
> One Boat for One Ship
> One Man for Ten of the Enemy
> or One Tank.

Battle of Motobu Peninsula

The following day Shepherd ordered the armored spearhead of the 4th and 29th Marines to attack north up the Ishikawa Isthmus toward the Motobu Peninsula, the 4th on the east coast road and the 29th on the west road, to sweep the northern end of the island. The regiments' advance was slowed by difficult terrain, poor roads, and fumbling enemy defense measures, which were almost amateurish. The emplaced obstacles were pushed away by tank-dozers or bulldozers. Mines were not laid properly and were not covered by infantry fire.

The 29th Marines encountered several English-speaking Okinawans who had lived in Hawaii. The Marines were told there was a concentration of one thousand Japanese in the Motobu Peninsula. The report was confirmed by combat patrols and aerial photo terrain studies that indicated the enemy had selected the Motobu Peninsula's rugged mountains for their final defensive position. The Okinawans said further that the Japanese 44th Independent Mixed Brigade, or *Kunigami* Detachment under Colonel Takehiko Udo, had prepared a well-organized defense system on the mountainous slopes of the one-mile-long, eight-mile-wide Motobu Peninsula. Udo's composite force was comprised of infantry (4th, 5th, and 6th Infantry Companies), 2nd Machine Gun Company, light and medium artillery, Okinawa home-guard conscripts (Iron and Blood Imperial Duty Corps *Tekketsu Kinnotai*), and naval personnel, some 15 hundred diehard fighters. Colonel Udo established his command post in a ravine on the towering 1,200-foot Mount Yae-Take, near the center of the peninsula, whose steep and broken terrain precluded the use of armor, leaving it to the infantry to dig out the defenders.

Initially, Shepherd believed the 29th Marines would be enough to eliminate Udo's force. The Japanese proved to be more than the one regiment could handle, however, and he ordered the 4th Marines, less 3d Battalion, into the fray. On April 13, the 29th Marines' attack was stopped by intense Japanese fire. Company A was ambushed and hit hard by 20-mm machine guns, suffering heavy casualties. Japanese counterbattery fire hit the supporting artillery positions of 2/15, destroying a 105-mm artillery howitzer, an ammunition dump, and inflicting 32 casualties. Air strikes were called in on suspected Japanese positions with unknown results.

Shepherd planned a two-pronged attack on April 14. The attack jumped off at 8:30 a.m. with the 3d Battalion, 29th on the left and 2nd Battalion, 4th on the right. They encountered stiff resistance. A battalion commander was killed and several company commanders wounded before reaching their objective, a 700-foot ridge west of Yae-Take. Marine casualties amounted to 109 killed, 375 wounded, and six missing. Eleven hundred enemy dead were counted. Meanwhile, 1st and 2nd Battalions, 4th Marines worked their way to the southwest corner of the peninsula in anticipation of a continuation of the attack. On April 15, the two regiments formed a continuous line around the south, east, and west sides of Mount Yae-Take, which brought them in position for the final assault.

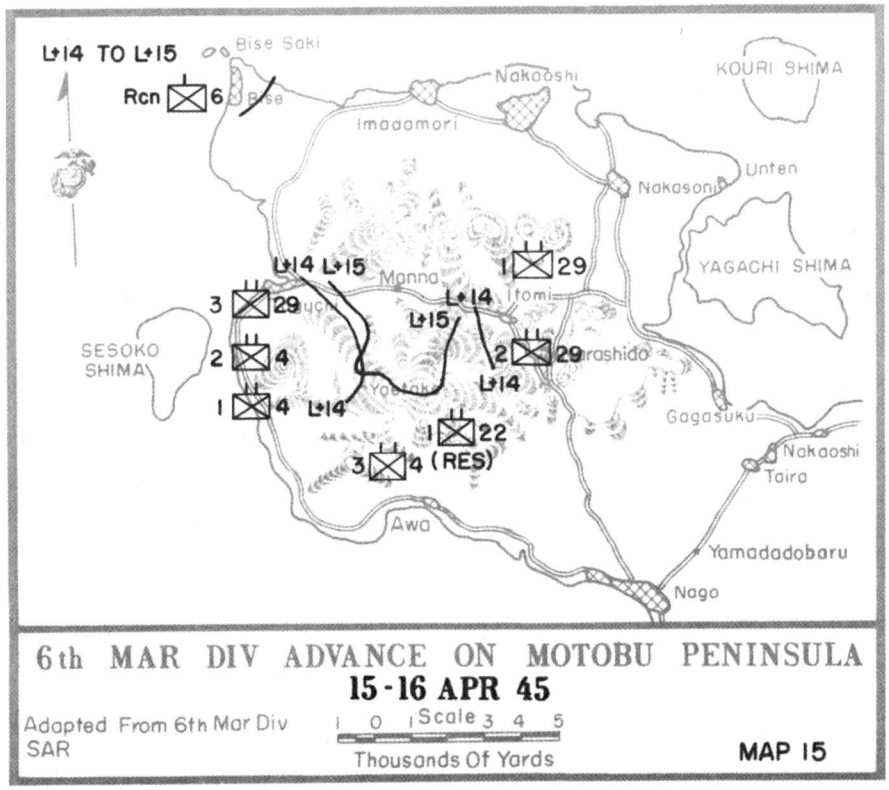

6th Marine Division advance on Motobu Peninsula. (U.S. Marine Corps)

Early on April 16, the 1st Battalion, 4th Marines, supported by planes, artillery, and naval guns, moved up the steep slopes of Yae-Take. Forward elements of the battalion climbed up the wooded slopes, apparently unobserved. As the Marines moved out on steep bare rock one hundred yards from the crest, knee mortar shells and hand grenades exploded on the face of the slope, forcing the troops to pull back into the woods. On the right (southeast) other troops of the battalion worked their way up a small valley under rifle fire. In a coordinated attack both forces charged over the summit and into the defending Japanese positions. By late afternoon the 1st Battalion had secured the crest, wiping out the defenders. Below them they could see the Japanese preparing to counterattack. The battalion called in heavy mortar and artillery fire, while replenishment ammunition was rushed to them. At 6:50 p.m. the expected charge came. The Marines held their ground in hand-to-hand combat against the banzai attack and killed more than three hundred attackers.

On April 17, the assault elements of the two regiments continued the attack and rapidly drove through the remaining Japanese defenders. Udo's main force was routed. The hastily departing enemy force left a scene of an undisciplined retreat, leaving behind seven hundred dead, military equipment, and large stores of food, weapons, and clothing. There was little doubt that the 6th Division had broken the back of enemy resistance on the peninsula.

The final drive to the northern coast of the peninsula began on April 18. The 4th and 29th Regiments swept forward against negligible resistance and on April 20 reached the north coast of the island. Shepherd declared that all organized resistance had ended. He believed the division had killed practically every Japanese on the peninsula. Patrol reports indicated, however, that some of the home-guard units that had escaped from the peninsula were preparing to fight as guerrillas. From April 20 until April 30, the division's combat patrols killed a few Japanese and home-guardsmen almost every night, but fewer as the days went by.

In driving the Japanese from the Motobu Peninsula, the 6th Marine Division suffered casualties: 236 killed, 1,061 wounded, and seven missing. The division took 46 prisoners and counted more than 25 hundred

Japanese bodies. The division also captured 11 field guns (75-mm and 150-mm), two six-inch naval guns, and large quantities of mortars, machine guns, and 20-mm antiaircraft guns.

Entering the Lists

On April 30, Shepherd received preparatory orders to move the division to join the Tenth Army on the southern part of the island, where General Mitsuru Ushijima had the bulk of his Thirty-Second Army. The Japanese had constructed a series of defensive positions that were almost impregnable. The ground was easily honeycombed with machine gun nests and fortified positions. Each one had to be overcome with tanks and supporting arms.

During the planning for the move, Shepherd asked Geiger if his division could go into line along the coast, the extreme west flank of the III Amphibious Corps' zone of action. He wanted this position to allow him to make maximum use of naval gunfire in his attack. General Geiger agreed, but when the order arrived, it tied his division to the advance of the 1st Marine Division, negating his freedom of maneuver. Shepherd approached Geiger again, who saw the sense in the request, and ordered the plan changed.

Service troops were the first element of the division to start south on May 2, quickly followed by the 15th and 29th Regimens the next day, with the 4th and the 22nd Regiments and the rest of the division on successive days. By the evening of May 6, the entire

General Mitsuru Ushijima, commanding general of the Thirty-Second Army. Shepherd considered him a "great" Japanese general. (Public Domain)

division was assembled around Chibana, about 10 miles north of the front lines. As the division trucked south, it passed convoys of Army troops headed away from the fighting. Flushed with victory, the Marines were contemptuous of the dispirited Army troops, particularly the 27th Division because of its mediocre performance on Saipan—Marine Lieutenant General Holland M. Smith relieved the 27th Division's commanding general, Major General Ralph C. Smith, in the middle of the battle for inability to lead his division. The relief caused a firestorm of bad feelings between the Army and Marines, which eventually fell on Holland's shoulders. It was thought that him not getting an invitation to the surrender ceremony on the *Missouri* at the end of the war was in retaliation.

Lieutenant General Isamu Chō, chief of staff, Thirty-Second Army. (Public Domain)

The division's move coincided with a period of heavy rain that continued for a week, completely saturating the ground and making it difficult for vehicles to move. The whole country became bogged down under deep and gummy mud. The infantry continued, however, to slog ahead through the morass.

Crossing the Asakawa River

On May 8, Shepherd designated the 22nd Marines to lead the division. He ordered it to move forward to the high ground overlooking the Asakawa River, the first heavily defended obstacle, and effect a relief of the 1st Marine Division's 7th Regiment.

The 22nd Regiment's 2nd Battalion was heavily shelled that night but did not suffer any casualties. The next day, the regiment conducted several patrols, which discovered that the high ground south of the river was held by the Japanese in strength. In addition, the river's estuary constituted a considerable barrier. Shepherd ordered the fabrication of a footbridge, which the 6th Engineers fabricated the next night under intermittent artillery fire. At 3:30 a.m., two companies of infantrymen from the 22nd Regiment raced across before the span was destroyed by a Japanese suicide team armed with satchel charges.

Just before dawn on May 10, as Shepherd watched from the 22nd Marines observation post, the 22nd Marines 1st and 2nd Battalions forced the river behind a smoke screen and, at day's end, had succeeded in gaining a bridgehead 14 hundred yards wide and four hundred yards deep on the south side of the river. They dug in for the night.

General Shepherd wanted to exploit the hard-won gains made on May 10 and ordered the 6th Engineer Battalion to construct a Bailey bridge so tanks could be pushed across to add heft to the advance. The engineers started fabricating the bridge under observed artillery and small arms fire, but by ten o'clock the next morning the bridge was completed. Shepherd thought the construction of the bridge "was a splendid feat of combat engineering. It was built under observed fire, both artillery and small arms."

A platoon of Sherman tanks rumbled across and homed in on the Japanese emplacements on the hillside. Point-blank fire from their 75-mm guns enabled the hard-pressed Marines to reach the top of the hill, but three of the Shermans were knocked out by mines. The stage was set for the 6th Division's drive toward a trio of mutually supporting low hills.

Sugar Loaf Hill

The first of the unassuming heights was dubbed Sugar Loaf Hill, the western anchor of the Japanese Shuri defense system. The 300-yard rectangular-shaped mound barely rose 50 feet out of the flat terrain. It was innocuously described as a "prominent hill" in Target Area 7672 G; however, the hill was so small it didn't show up on the standard military map with its 10-meter contour interval. Sugar Loaf, Half Moon Hill (220 feet high), and Horseshoe (190 feet high) were honeycombed

Sugar Loaf Hill. (USMC)

with tunnels, caves, and weapons positions. The three hills comprised a complex of mutually supporting defensive positions that took the 6th Marine Division 12 days to capture.

During the night of May 12–13, the Japanese attempted a counter-landing, which was broken up by naval patrol boats. Forty of the infiltrators made their way ashore but were killed by alert Marines.

The Battle for Sugar Loaf Hill

The 22nd Marines had taken a beating in the preceding three days, suffering eight hundred casualties, and its combat effectiveness had deteriorated. Shepherd ordered the 29th Marines to assume the main attack, supported by the 22nd on the right flank. The attack kicked off at 7:30 a.m. on May 14. The 29th Regiment attacked the crescent-shaped Half Moon Hill, while the 2nd Battalion, 22nd Marines launched a combined tank-infantry assault on the middle hill (Sugar Loaf). The two heights plus a third, Horseshoe, constituted the western anchor of the Japanese defense.

Resistance was strong and well-coordinated on the two hills. By late afternoon, the 29th was fighting at grenade range in the valley fronting Half Moon Hill, and the 22nd Marines' advance on Sugar Loaf Hill was brought to a complete halt. Major J. L. Courtney, executive officer of the 2nd Battalion, recognized the significance of the height and decided to launch an immediate attack in order to seize it. Shortly after dark, he led a small group of men up the slopes. They reached the top in time to stop a Japanese assault, but Courtney was killed in the process.

May 16 was considered to be the "Bitterest Day" of the Okinawan campaign for the 6th Division. Two regiments attacked the hill but were still not successful. They suffered staggering losses. General Shepherd and Lieutenant Colonel Krulak came forward in the late afternoon for their daily visit to the front. It was clear why the day's attack had not been successful: the Sugar Loaf defenses had been reinforced and strengthened during the past 24 hours and the intense enemy fire from the division's left and left rear would continue to be a serious threat until the Shuri area was reduced.

On May 18, however, a flanking movement brought a breakthrough. A small, almost imperceptible depression had been accidentally discovered by several Marines who had passed through it without taking too much fire—the Japanese were distracted by the fight on Sugar Loaf. The depression was east of the hill and ran north to south between Half Moon and Sugar Loaf.

Death of a Commander

On the afternoon of May 18, Shepherd was on his way to the front when he received word that the commander of the Tenth Army had been killed. "He was in my territory and I wanted to be there with him, so I hot-footed it up there to join him."[4]

General Buckner had gone forward to the front lines to watch the action. As he watched from the high ground near Mezado Ridge, a Japanese shell exploded nearby, shattering a concrete outcropping. A chunk of coral drove into Buckner's chest. Despite the efforts of the men around him, he died 10 minutes after being struck.

Shepherd had gotten to know Buckner quite well.

> During the hard fought battle for Shuri, where the Marine and Army Divisions lost so many men before capturing this important terrain feature, I tried to

persuade General Buckner to land the Second Marine Division, which was being held in Army Reserve, on the southeast coast of the island. In my opinion this would have forced the withdrawal of Japanese troops from Shuri to defend the beachhead established by 2nd Division, thereby weakening the strongly defended enemy line which extended from Conical Hill on the east coast to Sugar Loaf Hill on the west coast. If the Japanese did not contain this proposed landing, the 2nd Division which was still afloat with its 30-days resupply, would be in a position to attack Shuri from the south. But Buckner did not agree with my concept on the premise the Division could not be supplied. I told General Buckner that a Marine Division always carried with it a thirty day supply of food, ammunition, etc., and once their transports were unloaded, the Division could take care of itself.

I felt very strongly that if the Second Division was landed in rear of the Japanese lines, even if it only established and defended a beachhead line, it would require the Japanese to contain it, thereby weakening their main defense line which the remainder of the Tenth Army was having such a difficult time penetrating. But like so many Army officers, General Buckner did not cotton to amphibious operations and failed to see the versatility inherent in a Marine Task Force which is capable of landing at any point on an enemy coast line where the beaches are suitable for landing operations and sustaining itself for a limited period of time.

After the fighting was over and Okinawa declared secured, I made a trip to the particular area I had suggested for the landing of the Second Marine Division and found the beachhead area well suited for defense. If the Second Marine Division had been landed, it could have accomplished the mission of requiring Japanese troops to withdraw from their Shuri defenses and made it easier for the Tenth Army to capture the Shuri Hill mass.[5]

Buckner's death caused a great controversy over who would succeed him. General Geiger, III Amphibious Corps, was the most senior officer on the island. The Army was not to let him command, and Lieutenant General Joseph W. Stilwell was dispatched from China, where he was in command of the entire China–Burma–India Theater. Shepherd weighed in on the Smith-versus-Smith affair during an oral interview: "The Army was completely off-base. They just made an issue of [the relief] because of the intensity of feelings between the Army and the Marine Corps. Many Army officers were relieved from command when they didn't do what they were supposed to do. General Holland Smith was justified in relieving General Ralph Smith when he failed to exercise appropriate command of his division on Saipan." Shepherd went on to say, "The 27th was a National Guard division with me on Okinawa and they never amounted to a hill of beans—I don't think they were worth chucks."[6]

The last photograph of Lieutenant General Buckner (far right) before he was killed. (U.S. Government)

Within five days Stilwell assumed command of the Okinawan campaign. Nevertheless, General Geiger has the distinction of being the only Marine—and the only aviator of any service—to have commanded a field army, if only for five days.

The Fall of Sugar Loaf

Shepherd and Krulak discussed the new plan of attack on the Sugar Loaf complex with Colonel William J. Whaling, commanding officer of the 29th Regiment, on May 18. In a calculated risk, Shepherd decided the 29th would attack through the depression in column, supported by tanks, with two battalions striking Half Moon Hill and then holding, while supporting a third battalion's attack on Sugar Loaf's left flank.

The 29th launched the attack with tanks working their way through minefields under heavy fire. Six of them were disabled, but the remainder gained positions to be able to support the attack. Half the attack force advanced around the left of the hill, and the other half advanced around the right side. After an hour of heavy fighting, they seized the hill and dug in. Additional troops reinforced them and helped fight off an intense counterattack. The lines held, and on the morning of May 19, Sugar Loaf was securely in Marine hands.

During the 10-day period up to and including the capture of Sugar Loaf, the 6th Division lost 2,662 killed and wounded. The frontline regiments lost an additional 1,289 men due to exhaustion, sickness, and combat fatigue.

For several days after Sugar Loaf fell, the division continued to assault Half Moon Hill, but without success. The Marines were driven back off the crest several times. The Japanese were firmly dug in on the reverse slope. Shepherd decided to call off the attacks and instead leave a strong force on the western slope of Half Moon Hill to contain the enemy and prevent it from attacking the division's rear.

The Capture of Naha

On the night of May 21–22, a slow, drizzling rain began and continued for the next nine days, turning the entire area into an expanse of bottomless red mud. Despite the difficult conditions, Shepherd sent patrols from the 6th Reconnaissance Company across the lower Asato Gawa River. The patrols reported little enemy resistance. Based on their intelligence, Shepherd decided to force the river. Four companies of the 1st and 2nd Battalions, 4th Marines waded through the ankle-deep water under cover of smoke and established a firm beachhead on the south bank by midmorning of May 23.

As the day wore on the river rose because of the rain and became a chest-high torrent. Division engineers hurriedly constructed two footbridges, but a Bailey bridge was delayed by intense Japanese artillery fire until the afternoon of May 24. Later that night, a patrol from the Division Reconnaissance Company were sent across the river into Naha to see if it was held in strength. They found only occasional snipers. On May 25, Shepherd ordered an advance to clear the Japanese out of Naha,

Naha after bombardment. (U.S. Government)

and four days later the devastated city was free of the enemy. With Naha in hand, the 6th Division continued its southward movement with two regiments—the 22nd and 29th. By May 30, they had reached the high ground overlooking the Kokura River.

The Battle for Oroku Peninsula

Thus far Shepherd's division in 24 days of combat had suffered more than four thousand casualties. Ahead lay the Oroku Peninsula and its 5,000-man Okinawa Base Force garrison under Rear Admiral Minoru Ōta, a veteran Rikusentai officer.

The initial plan of the III Corps was to make a river crossing of the Kokuba Estuary. Shepherd considered it but decided that the Japanese planned their defense against this type of attack. Instead, he proposed his own plan to General Geiger. His plan for the division was to make an amphibious landing on the northwest coast of the two-by-three-mile peninsula in order to envelop the Japanese defenses from the west. Geiger approved the proposal.

Shepherd issued a warning order to the 1st and 2nd Battalions, 4th Marines to alert them for a possible amphibious assault on the Oroku Peninsula. The final plan prepared by the division staff in five days envisioned the division making an amphibious landing on the northwest coast of the peninsula across the Nishikoku Beach, just north of the Naha airfield. The 4th Marines would lead the assault, followed by the 29th Marines. Two companies of tanks would support the landings. The two battalions were to drive rapidly inland to seize the dominating terrain.

Rear Admiral Minoru Ōta. (U.S. Government)

Shepherd envisioned a pincer movement: the 4th and 29th Marines would push rapidly forward and by an encircling movement drive the enemy northeast toward the Kokuba Estuary. The 22nd Marines would cross the estuary and attack westward. Once contact was made between the three regiments, they would push forward northward, closing in on the Japanese in the vicinity of Oroku. The enemy couldn't escape across the Kokuba Estuary, and they would be either killed or captured in the final assault.

The plan also called for the capture of Ono Yama, the tiny island in the mouth of the Kokura Estuary. The 6th Reconnaissance Company, reinforced with an infantry company of the 29th Marines, made the landing under cover of darkness. By 8:00 a.m. only two Japanese had been located, and it was apparent that the island had been evacuated.

The company was also given the mission of gathering intelligence on Nishikoku Beach and Japanese strength on the peninsula. Four four-man teams paddled across the river at night in plastic boats, and after six hours deep in enemy territory the scouts returned. They reported that there was considerable enemy activity on the high ground north and east of the Naha airfield. The Reconnaissance Company commander estimated that the northern Oroku area was occupied but not in great strength. Other teams made a reconnaissance of Nishikoku Beach. They reported that the beaches were suitable for LVT landings and capable of supporting wheeled vehicles.

Geiger approved Shepherd's plan, and by 11:00 p.m. on June 3 all preparations were complete. Shepherd said that the Oroku landing "was a complicated affair: embarkation taking place under cover of darkness, the approach being made with inadequate aids to navigation, and no opportunity available for rehearsal or even a detailed briefing."[7]

Prior to the landing, the Oroku Peninsula erupted in flame and smoke under the pounding of hundreds of naval guns, artillery batteries, and aerial bombs. At one point, 15 artillery battalions fired a 30-minute preparation of more than 43 hundred rounds of high explosive ammunition that was placed on the high ground immediately fronting the landing beaches.

Shapley divided the 600-yard Nishikoku Beach between 2/4 on the left and 1/4 on the right, with the 29th Marines scheduled to land when the bridgehead was secure. Despite heavy rains, the assault went on schedule, with the two assault battalions landing at 5:51 a.m. despite intermittent machine gun and 20-mm fire. By 6:50 a.m. on June 4, 24 tanks and four M7 Priest self-propelled 105 howitzers were ashore and supporting the attack. General Shepherd and his chief of staff watched the assault from a bluff overlooking the Kokuba Estuary. Shepherd recalled, "To me, the final phase of this battle was one of the most interesting experiences of my military career. To be able to sit in a grandstand seat and watch the three infantry regiments of my Division attack toward me was a unique experience. Through my field glasses, I could see the men of the assault companies moving forward in their attack on the final Japanese defensive position."[8]

Shepherd related an interesting incident as he watched the last stage of the battle:

> An interesting incident occurred in the last stage of the battle. Several of the Japanese officers committed hari-kari on the beach opposite to where we were observing the final assault. We saw one Japanese officer take off his sword, lay it on top of a rock and blow himself up with a grenade. McQueen said to me, "I want that sword" and left immediately to cross over the Estuary by a bridge we had erected near Naha. By the time Johnny arrived at the spot where the Japanese officer had placed his sword on a rock, the sword had disappeared, apparently taken by one of the men of the attacking troops. The next day McQueen sent out a memorandum to the infantry regiments participating in the attack stating that he would give the man who had found the sword $100.00 for it. The Marine who found the sword turned it in a few days later and received Johnny's award of $100.00.[9]

By midafternoon the assault battalions had overcome the light resistance and were 15 hundred yards inland, including part of the Naha airfield. The bridgehead was secure enough to warrant the landing of the 29th Marines. The regiment went into the lines to the left of the 4th Marines. Based on the limited response of the Japanese defenders, the amphibious landing was considered to have achieved complete surprise.

By dark, the two regiments occupied 12 hundred yards of the Oroku Peninsula. During the night the lines were subject to intermittent mortar and spigot mortar fire, which the Japanese used as a psychological weapon intended to frighten more than inflict casualties. The mortar fire did not stop the two regiments from advancing on June 5, however, the 4th Marines on the right and the 29th on the left. Both regiments ran up against enemy strongpoints that delayed the advance. Nevertheless, the division's beachhead was deepened by one thousand yards and the Naha airfield was 90 percent captured.

Stiff enemy resistance on June 6 was centered on a ridge that ran along the length of the peninsula. Both regiments were held up in this area by automatic weapons, mortars, and rocket bombs. The terrain limited tank support—muddy fields and cratered roads were heavily mined. Hill 57, a high ridge in the 4th Regiment's zone, took two days to capture. The 29th Marines continued to meet stiff resistance in the vicinity of the town of Gushi from concealed caves in the coastal ridges.

The division intercepted and translated a message from Admiral Ōta to naval headquarters in Tokyo that gave an indication that the end of the battle was near. "The troops under my command have fought gallantly, in the finest tradition of the Japanese navy. Fierce bombardments may deform the mountains of Okinawa but cannot alter the loyal spirit of our men."[10] This was evidenced by a series of fruitless local counterattacks all along the front. After daylight more than two hundred dead Japanese were counted. On June 12, 86 enemy soldiers surrendered, the largest number captured thus far in the campaign.

The 6th Division continued to press the attack until June 14, which marked the completion of the Oroku operation. In the 14 days of heavy fighting, almost five thousand enemy soldiers were killed and nearly two hundred taken prisoner. The victory had not been without cost; 16 hundred Marines had been killed or wounded.

Capture of Ara Saki Peninsula

"Following the battle of Oroku and capture of its important airfield, the 6th Marine Division advanced southward along the west coast toward the southern tip of Okinawa."[11]

The 6th Division continued to mop up in the Oroku area and plan for its commitment on the southern front. Shepherd brought the 22nd Marines up from reserve and tasked them to continue the attack southward toward three successive fortified ridges, Mezado, Kuwanga and Kiyamu. Under cover of darkness in the pouring rain, the regiment passed through the 7th Marines, 1st Marine Division to the scrub-covered slopes of Mezado Ridge. Their attack was supported by heavy artillery, naval gunfire, and air. All day the assault went on, taking one cave position after another, in the face of machine gun, mortar, and small arms fire, until they reached the crest.

The attack resumed the next morning against Kuwanga Ridge. The 1st and 2nd battalions, 22nd Marines, supported by tanks, jumped off at 8:00 a.m. and by noon had seized the crest. Colonel Harold Roberts, the regimental commander, was forward watching the assault when he was killed by a sniper. Shepherd had warned him the previous evening,

"The end is in sight. For God's sake don't expose yourself unnecessarily."[12] By noon portions of the high ground had been seized. Casualties had been heavy, and by the afternoon, Shepherd ordered the 3d Battalion into the fight. He also brought the 4th Marines forward to continue the advance. On the morning of June 19, the regiment attacked and succeeded in penning the remaining enemy into an area five thousand yards square.

The two regiments, the 4th and the 29th, resumed the attack, overrunning the enemy positions. Many of the surviving Japanese started committing suicide, while many others surrendered. Ōta transmitted his final message to General Ushijima ("Enemy tank groups are now attacking our cave headquarters; the Naval Base Force is dying gloriously") and committed suicide, his duty done. The fight for the Ara Saki was over.

Shepherd recalled that "Col. Woodhouse had brought an American flag with him so when his battalion reached the Northern tip of Okinawa he raised this flag on the Northern tip. Well, he carried his flag with him until he was killed and then one of his officers continued to carry it until the Southern tip. So, when we were approaching the Southern tip of the island I arranged for the Second Battalion, same battalion that had raised the flag on the Northern tip to raise it on the Southern tip, which was done. The flag I think now is up at VMI."[13]

As the flag was being raised on a rough-hewn pole, a bugler came forward and blew the stirring notes of "Colors."[14]

At 10:27 a.m. on June 21 all organized resistance in the 6th Marine Division zone of action ceased, in the 82nd day of a campaign during which the division was actively engaged for 69 of them.

Imperial Japan's Capitulation

The last note of the bugle had hardly faded away before the division shipped out to return to Guam to rest and refit. After getting their encampment "squared away," Shepherd introduced his standard training regime to ready the division for the proposed Operation *Downfall*, the invasion of Japan. Before the training could get underway, however, the Japanese emperor announced the capitulation of Japan on August 15 and formally signed the document of surrender on September 2.

Admiral William Halsey requested a regiment of Marines to accompany the fleet for a landing in Tokyo Bay. Shepherd assigned the reconstituted 4th Marine Regiment because of its prewar history. The regiment had been forced to surrender to the Japanese when the Philippines capitulated in 1941. Its men had to endure captivity for four long years. Shepherd assigned Brigadier General William T. Clement, assistant division commander, to lead the regiment into Japan with Halsey. In an interesting sidenote, Clement was one of the last Marines to escape aboard a submarine when the Philippines fell. Shepherd flew to meet the "New Fourth" when they landed. "I'd been fighting [Japan] for three years and I wanted to see what the country was like."[15]

CHAPTER 17

North China, September–December 1945

Early in September, Shepherd received warning orders for a move to North China to accept the surrender of Japanese troops for the Chinese Central Government and to supervise the repatriation of Japanese military and civilians. The division, less the 4th Marines still in Japan, and a detachment of the 1st Marine Aircraft Wing moved to the Shantung Peninsula, occupying Tsingtao, known as "The Riviera of the Far East," nearby Tsangkou airfield on the southern coast, and the port of Chefoo on the northern coast.

The mission of the division was spelled out by Shepherd:

> Our mission is to land and occupy Tsingtao and the adjacent Tsangkou Airfield, and the port of Chefoo; to assist local authorities in maintaining order and in preventing disease and starvation; to release, care for, and evacuate recovered Allied military personnel and Allied internees; to cooperate with the Chinese Central Government forces; to accept, when necessary, local surrender of Japanese forces, as authorized by higher authority, and to assist the Chinese in effecting the disarming and confining of these forces.[1]

General Shepherd and a small staff arrived in Tsingtao aboard the destroyer escort USS *Newman* at dawn on October 11 to confer with Chinese officials and to make a detailed reconnaissance prior to the landing of troops. The *Newman* ran into a typhoon near Okinawa; it was, according to Shepherd, his "roughest experience at sea." Waves as high as forty feet and winds that reached above one hundred knots lashed the ship. The next day, in the early afternoon, the first of Transport Squadron 24's transports bringing the rest of the division docked at wharfs. The 6th

Reconnaissance Company landed first and moved through the crowded streets, lined with cheering, flag-waving throngs. The company secured the Tsangkou airfield, about 10 miles from the city, for the observation aircraft of VMO-6.

Shepherd opened his headquarters in the former Japanese naval headquarters building in Tsingtao on October 13, 1945. He was approached three days later by an emissary of the Communist commander in Shantung with an offer to assist the Marines in destroying the Japanese military forces and puppet army and in policing Tsingtao. It called attention to the fact that the Nationalist army was going to land at the city under the protection of the Marines in a move that was sure to bring open war in Shantung; despite this, the Communist general hoped that his force and the Marines could still cooperate. General Shepherd carefully prepared a point-by-point reply and dispatched it by the same emissary on October 16. The Marine commander pointed out that the mission of his division was a peaceful one and that it could not and would not cooperate in any way to destroy Japanese or Chinese forces. The city of Tsingtao was also peaceful, he noted, and, should any disorders arise, his division of "well-trained combat veterans" would be "entirely capable of coping with the situation."

Shepherd then stated that the movement of Nationalist troops into Tsingtao was a factor beyond his control, but that he could promise that the 6th Division would not take the part of either side in armed conflict. In the face of the Marine general's determination to carry out his orders to cooperate with the Nationalist government and to avoid assistance to Yenan's forces, the Communist commander could make no headway.[2]

Shepherd had Major General Nagano, commander of the Japanese 5th Independent Mixed Brigade, brought to his office prior to the official signing of the surrender documents in order for him to read it over and verbally agree to acceptance of the terms. Shepherd specified that his G-2 would meet him at noon with a staff car at a specified crossroads on the outskirts of Tsingtao. Shepherd's rationale for the escort was his concern that the Chinese might shoot him. Twelve o'clock came and went with no sign of the Japanese officer. Another 10 minutes went by.

The escort reported by radio, "Can't find the Jap general." Another half an hour went by and Shepherd was worried: "What will I do, if he doesn't show up?"[3]

Finally, an embarrassed Nagano arrived. There had been a mix-up on the crossroads. He had gone to the wrong place and waited there for the Marine escort. After several minutes and no Marines, Nagano decided to take his own car to Shepherd's headquarters.

Shepherd's chief of staff and an interpreter read through the surrender documents paragraph by paragraph. Nagano agreed to the terms, which stipulated that all Japanese troops in the area would be under Shepherd's command and would fight the Chinese Communists in the area. Shepherd questioned this provision, but he was overruled by the corps commander, General Keller Rockey, based on the decision of Generalissimo Chiang Kai-shek, the leader of the Republic of China.

The formal surrender of Major General Eiji Nagano's 10 thousand troops took place in an elaborate ceremony at the Tsingtao racecourse on October 25, 1945.[4] Shepherd and Lieutenant General Chen Pao-Tsang, Chiang's representative, took the surrender in the name of the Chinese Central Government. Nagano, his staff, and a battalion of Japanese troops were in formation at the appointed time. Shepherd had more than 12 thousand men of his division turned out—every vehicle, every artillery piece, and every tank in order to show both the Japanese and the Communists the strength and firepower of the division.

Shepherd demanded that the Japanese general surrender his sword as a symbol of his defeat. At the appointed time, Nagano came forward to the reviewing stand, unhooked his sword, placed it on the table in front of Shepherd, and signed the surrender documents. Following the signing, the division passed in review. The colorful ceremony lasted several hours.

The 6th Marine Division settled into a garrison routine with relative ease. The potential for trouble was strong in view of the fact that armed irregulars recognized by Chiang Kai-shek's Central Government were running the city, while the Communists, who held most of Shantung Province, controlled the countryside. Additionally, impoverished thousands of jobless refugees jammed the poorer sections of the city and overflowed into a miserable collection of shacks and cave hovels on

Surrender of Japan, Tsingtao, China, October 25, 1945. Aerial view of the Tsingtao racecourse during formal Japanese surrender to the 6th Marine Division, Tsingtao, China, October 25, 1945. (Official U.S. Marine Corps photograph, now in the collection of the National Archives)

its outskirts. A rash of thievery and mob action broke out from these slums, directed against German and Japanese households. The lawlessness occurred within a week of the Marine landing. The local police seemed powerless to prevent the outrages, but squad-sized patrols of the 22d and 29th Marines soon restored order. While the mob violence abruptly ceased with the advent of Marine street patrols, the threat of its renewal remained. General Shepherd's prompt action in bolstering civil authority had the desired effect, however. It dispelled any idea that may have existed in the minds of the people of Tsingtao, or of the watching Communists, that the 6th Marine Division was just a show force.

The first movement of repatriated Japanese military personnel started in mid-November, when three thousand naval personnel were loaded on three American LSTs, and continued until all the approximately sixty thousand Japanese troops were evacuated.

General Nagano called on Shepherd as he was about to return to the United States and presented him with two priceless samurai swords, one seven hundred years old, in appreciation for the courteous treatment Shepherd showed him and in feeding and taking care of his troops before they were evacuated back to Japan.

The samurai sword had been in the Nagano family for 350 years, and he asked Shepherd to treat it with respect. Shepherd tried to return the sword years later, but Nagano said he couldn't accept it.

Surrender of Japan, Tsingtao, China, October 25, 1945. Major General Eiji Nagano, commander of the Japanese Forces in the Tsingtao, China, area, lays his samurai sword on the table in front of Major General Lemuel C. Shepherd Jr., 6th Marine Division, and Lieutenant General Chen Pao-Tsang, commander of the Chinese forces, October 25, 1945. (Official U.S. Marine Corps photograph, now in the collection of the National Archives)

This act of surrender and all subsequent orders and proclamations of the Generalissimo, Chiang Kai-shek, to the surrendered forces will be issued at once to appropriate subordinate commanders and forces, and it will be the responsibility of all Japanese Commanders and forces to see that such proclamations and orders are immediately and completely complied with.

Any member of the forces surrendered hereby, who fails or delays to act in accordance with this act of surrender or future orders or proclamations of the Generalissimo, will be summarily and drastically punished, together with his responsible commanders.

We understand and acknowledge that the Commanding General, Sixth Marine Division, and the Deputy Commander, Eleventh China War Area, are the duly authorized representatives of the Generalissimo Chiang Kai-shek, and that we will immediately and completely carry out and put into effect his orders and instructions.

In case of conflict or ambiguity between the English text of this document and any translation thereof, the English text shall govern.

Signed at Tsingtao on the 25th day of October 1945 by Command and in behalf of the Emperor of Japan and the Japanese Government.

_____
        Nagano Eiji

_____
Accepted at Tsingtao on the __25th__ day of __October__ 1945 for China, the United States, Great Britain and the Union of Soviet Socialist Republics, and the interest of the other United Nations at war with the Japanese.

For the Generalissimo Chiang Kai-shek

_____
Major General, United States Marine Corps
Commanding, Sixth Marine Division

_____
Major General, Chinese Army
Deputy Commander Eleventh Chinese War Area

Instrument of Surrender. (U.S. Government)

In contrast to the extended deployment of the 1st Division in Hopeh, the 6th Division had no security responsibility for communication routes in the interior of Shantung. With the exception of the rifle company regularly on guard at Tsangkou airfield, no unit of General Shepherd's command held a position exposed to Communist harassing attacks. However, Shepherd requested Marine Aircraft Group 32 (MAG-32) to conduct daily search and reconnaissance missions over eastern Shantung Peninsula to keep track of Communist activity against Tsingtao and the progress of Japanese units moving toward the repatriation port.

Aerial surveillance reports indicated the Japanese were fully cooperating with the repatriation, which kept the requirement for Marine escorts and guard personnel low. Once it was well established ashore, the 6th Division easily met these demands that hardly taxed its strength, and it could operate at little more than idling speed.

The aerial surveillance was not without cost, however. On December 8, MAG-32, in a show of strength on the anniversary of Pearl Harbor, launched three squadrons. On their way back to the airfield, Marine Scout Bombing Squadron 343 ran into foul weather and lost six planes that crashed into mountain slopes in a blinding snowstorm. An immediate search of the area was launched, but it wasn't until three days later that Chinese villagers brought word of survivors. Shepherd sent out a recovery detail that was able to pick them up.

On December 11, a photo reconnaissance aircraft from Marine Photographic Squadron 254 crash-landed on a beach, but the crew escaped uninjured. The 6th Division dispatched Company F, 29th Marines with air and ground attachments to attempt to recover the aircraft. Soft ground prevented it from taking off, and it was stripped of usable parts and the carcass burned. The local villagers in both cases were cooperative.

General Shepherd realized that one of his major problems in Tsingtao was keeping his men usefully occupied. So long as the Communists posed no serious threat to the city and the repatriation process ran smoothly, there was a good chance that combat troops might lose efficiency. Idleness, even that of a relative nature, can be a curse to a military organization geared to operate at full capacity. In order to maintain unit standards of discipline, appearance, and performance, Shepherd instituted a six-week training program on November 12 that emphasized review of basic military subjects. The division commander also directed that each unit schedule at least 10 classroom hours a week for the study of academic and vocational subjects, to be held concurrently with the military training schedule.

On December 13, 1945, III Amphibious Corps notified Shepherd to disband the 6th Marine Division. It would shrink into the 3d Marine Brigade (reinforced), with its infantry component organized around the skeletonized 4th Marines, under the command of Major General Archie B. Howard.

Shepherd was detached from command of the 6th Marine Division at Tsingtao the day before Christmas 1945 in a formal ceremony. The division band played "Auld Lang Syne" as the general's personal flag was lowered from its staff.

CHAPTER 18

Assistant Commandant, March 1946–April 1948

Four days later Shepherd arrived in Washington and reported to General Alexander A. Vandegrift, the commandant, who told him that he was going to command the 2nd Marine Division. Instead, Shepherd was sent to Little Creek near Norfolk to organize Troop Training Unit (TTU), Atlantic, to teach both Army and Marine Corps units amphibious techniques. This was the third unit he had to organize from the ground up: 9th Marines, 1st Provisional Marine Brigade, and now the TTU. He struggled with this last assignment because there was no staff to help him. A "distress" call to Vandegrift brought some personnel relief, and Shepherd was able to "get the show on the road." This assignment was brief, and after three months he was ordered back to Headquarters Marine Corps to be both assistant commandant and chief of staff.

Shepherd thought the commandant viewed the chief of staff position as the senior billet and the assistant commandant served only as the standby for when the commandant was away: "He just signed the Commandant's mail." The assistant commandant did not have any specific duties or responsibilities in the organization of headquarters. There was no general staff system; each division worked separately, had its own function, and more or less operated directly under the commandant. The organization was a department system that was basically unchanged since the Spanish-American War.[1] However, General Shepherd kept his finger on the pulse of headquarters and provided guidance when necessary.

It was during this Washington tour that Shepherd first met the sculptor Felix de Weldon, who at the time was working on a monument that was a reproduction in bronze of the Iwo Jima flag raising. The Marine Reserve Officers Association had entered into a contact with De Weldon for the statue, which was estimated to cost about $350,000. Unfortunately, the association was able to raise only half the cost, so Shepherd took over the fundraising project. He considered the erection of the memorial statue a vital Corps project. He sent two personal letters to all active duty and retired officers asking for contributions. His plea was rewarded, and De Weldon was able to finish the project.

He visited De Weldon's studio and was greatly impressed by the model of a proposed monument inspired by Joe Rosenthal's famed photograph of five Marines and one Navy hospital corpsman raising the flag over Mount Suribachi on Iwo Jima.

Iwo Jima Monument, Washington, D.C. (Photo by Lance Corporal Allen Sanders)

The selection and acquisition of a suitable piece of land was another difficult problem. There were no sites in Washington, D.C., so Shepherd and De Weldon picked a location across the Potomac River close to Arlington Cemetery known as the "Nevis Tract," which was owned by the government. The District of Columbia Fine Arts Commission approved the proportions and design of the statue. The negotiations took months of discussion and pressure by friends of the Marine Corps. The Marine Corps War Memorial was dedicated at an impressive ceremony attended by the president of the United States and a number of government officials as well as a number of Marine officers and civilian supporters of the Corps. Shepherd gave the dedication address, and the vice president accepted the statue for the government. The Marine Corps War Memorial has become one of the greatest tourist attractions in Washington region. On Tuesday evenings during the summer the Marine Barracks Washington, the oldest post of the Corps, puts on a sunset parade.

Shepherd felt strongly that the Corps should have an official Marine Corps seal, so he called on De Weldon for assistance in the design, which resulted in the present-day seal—a Marine ornament in a circular background with the words "Department of the Navy" above the ornament. The outside perimeter of the circular background is a corded piece of rope symbolic of the Corps' seagoing service.

Shepherd took a red and gold plaster of Paris model to President Eisenhower for approval. He liked the design and inscribed it with his signature. Bronze castings were distributed to posts and stations throughout the Corps. Shepherd also asked De Weldon to redesign the American eagle to be used on all Marine uniform ornaments. Previously, many uniform ornament manufacturers had used their own design.

During a meeting of NATO on November 18, 1955 when he was commandant, Shepherd visited Belleau Wood and found there wasn't a single marker showing that the Marines had captured the place or that it had been named "Bois de la Brigade de Marine."

Seal of the United States Marine Corps. (U.S. Government)

Belleau Wood bas-relief. (Defense Visual Information Distribution Service)

The lack of any recognition upset him, so when he returned to the United States, he was determined to rectify the oversight. He sent out a plea to all the Corps officers asking them to contribute a dollar for a monument. Next he asked Felix de Weldon, who had been instrumental in the Iwo Jima Monument in Arlington, to design a small monument with a suitable plaque. Shepherd believed the finished statue, a bas-relief in bronze on a black granite slab, to be a fitting memorial to the Marines who fought there.

De Weldon designed a bronze bas-relief figure of a Marine charging with a fixed bayonet. The base of the stone shaft and the

General Lemuel C. Shepherd Jr., then commandant of the Marine Corps, returned after 37 years to Belleau Wood, where he had fought as a lieutenant during World War I, to deliver the major address dedicating the monument (covered by flag) to the 4th Brigade of U.S. Marines and their gallantry during the Belleau Wood encounter of 1918. (Official photograph from the archives of the Marine Corps History Division)

base of the monument were sculpted of Swedish black granite. Shepherd prepared a brief inscription listing the units of the 4th Marine Brigade that had participated in the battle and a notation that the name of "Belleau Wood" had officially been changed by the French government to "Bois de la Brigade de Marine." Shepherd took great pride in having initiated and accomplished the erection of the monument.

CHAPTER 19

Battle of the Potomac, May 1948

U.S. Marines Fight for Survival, Defense Unification 1944–1947

Army Chief of Staff General George C. Marshall fired the opening round in the unification battle on November 2, 1943, with a memorandum to the Joint Chiefs of Staff calling for "a single department of war in the post war period." In the ensuing heated discussions and debates, as outlined in JCS 1478 papers and Senate Bill 2044, the War Department intended to see the role of the Corps severely reduced. In the plan, the Marines would fight "only in minor shore combat operations in which the Navy alone is interested." Its size would be limited to "lightly armed units, no larger than a regiment, to protect American interests ashore in foreign countries, and to provide interior guard of naval ships and shore establishments." The total strength of the Corps would be limited to 60 thousand with no expansion in time of war, the Marine Corps reserve would be abolished, and Marine units would be held below the size requiring the combining of arms. Marine aviation would be merged into naval aviation or be transferred to the Air Force. Finally, Marines were to be restricted to the "waterborne aspects of amphibious operations" (duty as landing craft crews and beach labor parties).[1]

These recommendations would have reduced the Marines to little more than a naval palace guard. Since the Marine Corps, which had topped 485 thousand only a year before, was to be restricted from expanding in time of war, there would be no requirement for a reserve force or aviation and artillery. The service primarily responsible for developing amphibious doctrine, the "key to World War II," would serve as landing craft crewmen and beach labor parties.

General Vandegrift and his assistant commandant, Lem Shepherd, immediately went to "general quarters!" They were afraid that the Marine Corps would be gobbled up by the Army. The most able officers in the Marine Corps were assembled and placed on a committee, called the Edson Board after Brigadier General Merritt A. Edson (Medal of Honor recipient and Guadalcanal hero), to come up with ideas. "The Army wanted to absorb us, and they would have absorbed us, I feel, if we hadn't fought them right down the line," Shepherd recalled. "We'd have lost our independence.... We would eventually have been washed out of the picture."[2]

The commandant appointed a panel in January 1947 under Shepherd to find a solution to the far-reaching problem of conducting amphibious operations in the atomic age. Shortly thereafter, Vandegrift decided to expand and further refine unification activities by appointing a special advisory group. The group was officially called the Board to Conduct Research and Prepare Material in Connection with Pending Legislation, although it may be properly called the Edson–Thomas board.

A loose-knit group of devoted junior officers was also formed under the leadership of Colonel Merrill B. Twining at Henderson Hall "to watch unification developments." They moved to Marine Corps Schools (MCS) Quantico, Virginia, where they could work and not be right under the gun from Washington. This MCS group was designated Research Section, Marine Corps Schools and dubbed the "Chowder Society," short for "Little Men's Chowder and Marching Society." Chowder's membership fluctuated from three or four to as many as 10. Its mission was to provide reports, studies, and recommendations to the commandant.

No Bended Knee

Senate Bill 2044 would have permitted "the Secretary of Defense to prescribe by fiat, without Congressional check, the roles and missions of the Armed Forces. The bill would have removed the Marine Corps from the protection of Congress and enable the War Department to institute its plan by the stroke of a staff officer's pen."[3]

On May 6, 1946, General Vandegrift appeared before the Senate Naval Affairs to give his views of Senate Bill 2044. Known as the "Bended Knee Speech," it was received favorably by the nation, forcing Congress to adjourn without taking action. Shepherd recalled, "There was a great deal of controversy, and the Corps came in for considerable criticism. There were those perhaps who were willing to sacrifice, knuckle down." This was not the end of the matter, however, only a reprieve. President Truman drafted an executive order "containing language of the most narrow and limiting character regarding the function of the Marine Corps."[4] At the same time, he ordered the secretary of the Navy to forbid all Navy and Marine officers from criticizing the bill.[5]

General Edson felt so strongly about the bill that he sacrificed his career by immediately retiring so that he could refute the president's executive order. His public and congressional testimony garnered positive results in the form of the National Security Act of 1947.[6] The act protected the Marine Corps as an independent service under the Department of the Navy. The act also provided for Fleet Marine Forces and confirmed the Corps' mission of seizing and defending advanced bases, as well as land operations in support of a naval campaigns.

Vandegrift was due to retire on January 1, 1948. Shepherd was a leading contender to be the next commandant, but so was Major General Clifton B. Cates, at that time the commanding general at Quantico. Their careers had been remarkably parallel. Both had heroic records as platoon leaders and company commanders in World War I. Both had been distinguished regimental and division commanders in World War II.

The two had been friends for many years, and, according to Shepherd, neither one was particularly interested in becoming involved in the unification fight that was going on at the time. Both of them would have liked to be commandant, but they were not making any unusual effort to take the job.

One morning the two of them were invited to have lunch with Secretary of the Navy John Sullivan. He told them that their names and records, along with those of several others, had been submitted to

President Truman for his decision on who would be the next commandant. That afternoon the president summoned them to the Oval Office to discuss who would take Vandegrift's place. Truman indicated that he had reviewed their records, and he noted that both were well qualified for the position. He went on to say that, as a military man himself (Truman had served as an Army artilleryman in World War I), he believed in seniority. He then told them that Cates, being senior and three years older, would be the next commandant, and that he would appoint Shepherd to follow him.

The Key West Agreement

In March 1948, Secretary of Defense James V. Forrestal and the service chiefs met in Key West, Florida, to settle their roles and missions. Commandant Cates was not invited. The agreement that emerged included the decision that, in the event of war, only four Marine divisions would be allowed, fewer than the six fielded during World War II and far fewer than Marine mobilization capability. Also, no tactical command above corps level would be permitted. Though hardly necessary given the other limitations, the agreement prohibited the Marines from creating a second land army.

General Cates protested in vain that making such decisions without his participation violated the intent of the 1947 National Security Act and harmed the ability of the Marine Corps to fulfill its amphibious mission. The committee ignored his protest, however, and decided that the Corps' expertise in amphibious warfare was "not considered essential."

Unhappy with the pace of defense budget cuts, President Truman jumped into the fray by firing Forrestal and replacing him with Louis A. Johnson, an ambitious political crony and former assistant secretary of war who "made Cliff Cates' life miserable by treating him with contempt … and hatred."[7]

Johnson planned to cut the Marine Corps and transfer its troops to the Army and its aviation to the Air Force. "Johnson severely hurt the Corps. In fiscal year 1949, he cut the FMF by 14 percent … in fiscal year 1950 by another 5 percent. He also planned by 30 June 1950 to cut another

19 percent. In addition, he ordered a 48 percent reduction in Marine Corps air strength. In sum, in two years he cut the Corps by a third."[8]

On August 29, 1950, the president continued the assault with a letter to Congressman Gordon L. McDonough, a staunch right-wing Republican foe: "The Marine Corps is the Navy's police force and as long as I am President that is what it will remain." And then he went on to say, "They have a propaganda machine almost the equal of Stalin's." His remark was picked up by the media and resulted in the largest outpouring of mail received by the White House during Truman's presidency. A week later, President Truman was forced to apologize, and in a letter to General Cates he wrote, "I sincerely regret the unfortunate choice of language which I used in my letter of August 29 to Congressman McDonough concerning the Marine Corps."

Shepherd, still a major general, left Headquarters Marine Corps in April 1948 to become commandant of Marine Corps Schools at Quantico. Cates and Shepherd had agreed that whichever of them was selected as commandant, the other would go to Quantico, because they both loved the base.

General Shepherd's arrival at Quantico caused a sudden and enthusiastic revival of his interest in horseback riding. The post stable at that time was across the parking lot from Breckinridge Hall near the railroad underpass. Gracias, a gray mare, was General Shepherd's favorite horse, and when she died, she was buried near the back gate, with a bronze plaque marking the grave. Despite being an excellent rider, Shepherd suffered an unfortunate accident when he fell off a horse. He was kicked in the head, which gave him a concussion. In later years he claimed that it made it difficult to remember things, and he was concerned that he might say something that would not be correct.

CHAPTER 20

Fleet Marine Force, Pacific, June 1950

Police Action Korean War

Shepherd stayed at Quantico until June 15, 1950, when he was notified to take command of Fleet Marine Force, Pacific (FMF-PAC), a three-star billet, with headquarters at Pearl Harbor, Hawaii. FMF-PAC was the senior billet in the Pacific and commanded the largest field command in the Marine Corps. He had to assume command by dispatch in order to get the three stars of a lieutenant general. Before he took the post, Shepherd was granted a month's delay by the commandant and Admiral Arthur W. Radford, commander in chief, Pacific Fleet, before reporting to his new duty station. He planned a leisurely automobile trip cross-country with his wife and aide, visiting friends and indulging in one of his favorite pastimes, fly-fishing. The chief of fisheries in Washington had authorized him to fish in Yellowstone Park's Lake Pearl, which was closed to the general public.

On June 25, the Shepherds reached Colorado Springs, where they spent the night. At breakfast the next morning, Shepherd picked up the local paper and learned of the North Korean attack. In a coast-to-coast coordinated attack in the predawn hours, the In Min Gun (North Korean People's Army) brushed aside the ineffective resistance of the Republic of Korea frontier force. Within three days the invaders seized Seoul, the capital, 35 miles south of the 38th parallel, forcing the government to flee, and turned its citizens into refugees desperate to escape the fighting. The North Korean People's Army was executing its operational plan, which called for advances of 15 to 20 kilometers a day, with main military operations completed within 22 to 27 days.

The United Nations Security Council met in an emergency session and declared North Korea's aggression a breach of the peace and demanded their immediate ceasefire and withdrawal. Two days later, after hearing nothing from the North Koreans, the Security Council passed another resolution, calling upon UN members to provide economic and military assistance to embattled South Korea. The United Nations was in the fight.

Acting quickly, President Harry S. Truman ordered American naval, air, and ground forces into action. The first contingents to arrive were hastily assembled occupation troops from Japan. They were understrength, soft from occupation duty, and short on heavy weapons and equipment. Shepherd considered, "In retrospect the Army had a couple of 'makee-learnee' divisions in Japan. It was during the Occupation period. The men were living in the lap of luxury in Japan. They weren't worrying about any war. A lot of them had come in after World War II, and had no combat experience—and there were very few veterans there."[1]

The American formations were immediately thrown into battle against the North Korean advance. They were chewed up by the tougher, Soviet-trained and Soviet-equipped Army, who totally outfought the unprepared and ill-equipped Americans. Shepherd felt there was a definite quality difference in the opposing forces. "They [U.S. forces] were not trained soldiers. All of a sudden they were thrown into battle against a strong enemy. These North Koreans were fighters and had successfully overrun South Korea. I can't blame or criticize the Army too much—they just were not prepared for combat against a determined enemy."[2]

Since Korea was in the Far Eastern theater under command of General Douglas MacArthur and not included in the Pacific Ocean area under Navy control, Shepherd assumed there would be no immediate requirement for the deployment of the Fleet Marine Force, Pacific. He continued his trip, and by the time his party reached the park, the war was heating up, so he notified his boss, Admiral Radford, that he was continuing his trip according to the itinerary but that if he was needed, he would cut short his leave and go to Hawaii by plane rather than by boat. Early the next morning he checked the local telegraph office but didn't find any message ordering him to cut short the leave.

Shepherd and his aide rented a boat and started on the long-awaited fishing excursion. They had just gotten about one hundred yards offshore when a girl came down the beach waving a telegram from Admiral Radford, directing him to proceed by air to Pearl Harbor. Shepherd canceled the remainder of his leave, packed his bags, and left for Salt Lake City, the nearest airport. He sent a telegram requesting a Marine aircraft to take him and his aide to San Francisco, where he caught a commercial flight to Honolulu.

As he stepped off the plane, he was met by his chief of staff, Colonel Gregon Williams, with a copy of a dispatch that had just been received from the commandant of the Marine Corps. It directed Shepherd to form a provisional brigade from units of the 1st Marine Division stationed at Camp Pendleton, California, and mount it out for Korea at the earliest possible date.

As commanding general of Fleet Marine Force, Pacific, Shepherd was directly in the administrative chain of command for the Marine units in Korea, responsible for their personnel and logistical support. "I felt it was my responsibility to insure that the 1st Marine Division received its replacements of personnel and supplies," he recalled.[3] He believed that "all Marines in the Pacific should be under the command of the Commanding General, Fleet Marine Force, Pacific." He was able to convince General Cates, and his command of all Marines in the Pacific became a fait accompli.

General Lemuel C. Shepherd Jr. reviews troops in Korea, 1953. (Virginia Military Institute)

In regard to personnel, Shepherd noted on one of his frequent trips to Korea:

> There was a considerable loss of personnel due to the evacuation to the United States of men with minor wounds who, with a month's rest could return to their units. With the scarcity of replacements ... I felt we couldn't afford, just because a man had a minor wound, to let him go back to the States. We'd probably never see him again. So, I instituted a Rest and Rehabilitation Camp near Kyoto. We were able to get a large hotel ... and I organized a regular R-and-R center there. In other words, a man came out of the hospital with mild wounds; he would go down there for rehabilitation, and spend a month or whatever time necessary to get back on his feet, and from there, back to duty in Korea as replacements.[4]

Shepherd was faced with a great many problems that had to be worked out in a short period of time. There was no contingency plan to deal with the Korean emergency, and there was only a small staff that he had never worked with. He took over command of FMF-PAC when the Marine Corps and the other services had been reduced to the very minimum under Secretary of Defense Lewis Johnson's budget cuts. Shepherd recounted that "Johnson had no use for the Corps. He cut us down to 70,000 troops, spread all over the world. We had the 1st Division, but it was woefully understaffed. Everything had been slashed tremendously. The Corps was about to go out of existence."[5]

At the start of the war, the Corps had difficulty finding enough Marines to form a war strength brigade, with its equipment and supplies together with supporting air units for combat. Marine regiments had been cut from three to two battalions and companies from four to three platoons at reduced strength. The artillery battalion had four 105-mm howitzers per battery rather than the normal six.[6] A few miles up the road at Marine Corps Air Station, El Toro, the 1st Marine Aircraft Wing was doing the same thing. Brigadier General Thomas J. Cushman formed Marine Aircraft Group (MAG) 33, consisting of four squadrons: Marine Fighter Squadron (VMF-214), VMF-323, VMF (Night Fighter)-513, and VMO-6, an observation squadron, which included four HO3S-1 helicopters and four OH light observation aircraft.[7]

The majority of Navy transports and cargo ships had been placed in "mothballs," thus preventing their immediate dispatch to ferry Fleet

Marine Forces from their bases in the United States to the Far East for employment in Korea.[8]

On July 1, 1950, the chief of Naval Operations queried Admiral Arthur W. Radford, commander in chief of the U.S. Pacific Fleet, about how soon a reinforced battalion or reinforced regiment from the 1st Marine Division could be ready to embark for duty in the Far East Command. Radford, following consultations with Shepherd, replied the same day that a battalion could sail in six days and a regiment in 10.

In anticipation of orders to come, Shepherd sent a warning order on July 2 to Brigadier General Edward A. "Eddy" Craig, the officer Shepherd had designated to command the 1st Marine Brigade, directing him to be prepared to embark a brigade for combat duty in the Far East Command. Craig had his work cut out for him. The division was seriously undermanned, and he had to nearly strip the 1st Marine Division in order to field the 5th Marines (reinforced), an understrength infantry regiment.

Shepherd's staff, under the guidance of the G-3, Colonel Victor H. "Brute" Krulak, prepared Operation Plan 2-50, dated July 5, 1950, covering embarkation, equipment, and supplies. The plan was carried to Camp Pendleton by officer courier. The plan ground elements were designated as the "1st Provisional Marine Brigade," under Craig, and the air elements "Marine Aircraft Group 33 (Reinforced)," under Brigadier General T. J. Cushman. Later MAG-33 was changed to "Forward Echelon, 1st Marine Aircraft Wing." Cushman was also designated deputy brigade commander. The brigade was formally activated on July 7, 1950. Several days after Shepherd arrived in Hawaii, Admiral Radford directed him to fly to Japan in company with Vice Admiral Thomas Sprague, U.S.N., commander of the Naval Air Force Pacific, for a conference with General MacArthur. The two officers and principal staff members arrived in Tokyo on the afternoon of July 9 and reported to Vice Admiral Turner Joy, U.S.N., commander U.S. Naval Forces Far East, who briefed them on the current situation in Korea.

The next morning, they were escorted to MacArthur's headquarters located in the Dai-Ichi Building, opposite the grounds surrounding the emperor's palace. They were greeted by Major General Edward M.

"Ned" Almond, MacArthur's chief of staff and a fellow "ring knocker" of Shepherd's from VMI, who escorted them into MacArthur's office. "I did have a number of Army people in the Far East Headquarters," Shepherd acknowledged. "During my two years' experience overseas with the Army in World War II, I met a lot of Army people, and I didn't have the antagonism towards them that a lot of Marines did." Among Marines, MacArthur was known as "Dugout Doug," a derisive nickname he was given because he and his staff and family were ensconced in tunnels on Corregidor. Shepherd did not support that. "He respected the Army general and thought MacArthur was a great leader … a fearless, courageous man."[9]

Always the gracious host, MacArthur welcomed Shepherd as an old comrade in arms. The two had met in Australia, where Shepherd was serving as assistant division commander, 1st Marine Division, then assigned to MacArthur's command. "With his fantastic memory, General MacArthur apparently recalled me personally as he greeted me warmly and began conversing about the landing at Cape Gloucester on Christmas Day."[10] "We had a lengthy conversation in his office," Shepherd reported. "You know he always wanted to talk. My God, talk, talk, talk, forty minutes, telling me all his experiences. We talked about Korea, we talked about this and that, and as we got up to go, he very courteously—he was always very courteous—he got up and went to the door of his office." A large map of Korea hung next to the door. MacArthur put his hand on Shepherd's shoulder and pointed, with the stem of his ever-present pipe, to a spot on the map adjacent to Seoul on the west coast of the peninsula. "Lem, if I had that 1st Marine Division as I had on Cape Gloucester, I'd land here at Inchon, seize Seoul, and cut the North Korean lines of communication."[11]

Shepherd was not taken aback; he had been thinking about the commitment of Marines a great deal:

> During my flight from Honolulu to Tokyo, I had given considerable thought to the operational command status of the 1st Marine Brigade upon its arrival in Korea. I feared that the Brigade, which was only a reinforced regiment at reduced strength, would probably be attached or integrated into an Army Division thus losing its identity as a Marine organization. Furthermore, I felt certain that

the Marine aircraft and helicopter squadrons which formed an integral part of a Marine Air-Ground Team would be assigned to the Far Eastern Air Force Command. My apprehension was based on attempts by the Army and Air Force to dismember the Marine Corps and reduce its roles and missions during discussions of the recently enacted "Unification of the Services" legislature. To insure that the Marine Units in Korea would be under command of a Marine General Officer of sufficient rank to protect the interests of the Corps, I had determined to suggest to General MacArthur that he request a Marine Division be sent to Korea. The First Marine Division, stationed at Camp Pendleton was under my administrative command and I felt with a first class war developing in the Far East that the Marine Corps, as the Nation's Force in Readiness, should be represented by a Marine Division supported by a Marine Air Wing. Anticipating General MacArthur's approval of my proposal I had drafted, during my flight to Tokyo, a carefully prepared dispatch to the JCS for General MacArthur's signature, which I brought with me to my conference with him on July 10th. This was the dispatch reference to above which "I took from my pocket" and rewrote on a message blank in Almond's office for General MacArthur's approval and transmitted to Washington.[12]

Shepherd suggested that MacArthur ask for the 1st Marine Division to be assigned to the Far Eastern Command. He pointed out that, while the division was under his operational command, he couldn't order it to Korea without the concurrence of General Cates and the authority of the Joint Chiefs of Staff. MacArthur asked him if he would take the matter up with General Cates. Shepherd responded that he believed General Cates would support his recommendation if MacArthur could obtain the approval of the Joint Chiefs of Staff for the assignment of the 1st Marine Division and 1st Marine Aircraft Wing to the Far Eastern Theater.

MacArthur then asked Shepherd to write a dispatch to the Joint Chiefs of Staff requesting the assignment of the entire 1st Marine Division and 1st Marine Aircraft Wing to the Far Eastern Command. Shepherd took his leave and went to the chief of staff's office to write the message. After working over several drafts, he selected the one that appeared to be suitable and took it in to MacArthur, who signed it and directed General Almond to send it off. The Joint Chiefs turned the request— and three more—down before finally approving the fifth message.

Shepherd found MacArthur "enthusiastic" about the prospect of employing the 1st Marine Division again. He had relied on it seven years before in the New Britain operation. He planned to stabilize the front in Korea as soon as possible as a prelude to the landing in the rear of the North Korean People's Army, which he believed would be decisive.[13]

Shepherd's next task was to convince the commandant, General Cates, that it was the right thing to do. He met Cates at Camp Pendleton, where he was visiting the brigade troops prior to their departure for Korea. Cates was somewhat put out with Shepherd for committing his Marines without consulting him. Fortunately, the two general officers were friends of long standing, or it could have turned out badly. Shepherd pleaded his case. "Clifton, you can't let me down on this. This is a hot war. We ought to be in it."[14] Cates responded, "We haven't got the men, we haven't got the men." But Shepherd won the day: "Clifton, we're fighting a hot war over there in Korea. NATO is something they're just forming on paper. We belong in the Pacific. The Western Pacific is our theatre." Cates finally gave the commitment his full backing. Colonel Victor Krulak, Shepherd's G-3, described the meeting: "I remember there was a pretty spirited dialogue at Camp Pendleton between General Cates and General Shepherd … about what we could or couldn't do. Neither General Shepherd nor I was very popular at that time because we had obviously overextended. We did exactly the right thing. We marched to the sound of the guns."[15]

Temper, Temper

Shepherd also met with his old friend Brigadier General Craig. "It was a complete surprise to me when he greeted me rather coldly and wanted an immediate conference with me at headquarters," Craig said. "On arrival he took off in a temper telling me that I had put him in a difficult position by requesting additional shipping after he had already given the Navy our requirements." Shepherd "chewed" him out for taking too many vehicles. "He said I would not need them … the brigade was only going to Japan to wait for the rest of the division …

and then be absorbed by it. He also complained that I was taking too many key members of the division to staff the brigade and finally, he was critical of my request for an additional rifle company to fill up the 5th Marines."

Craig tried to justify his requirements, but Shepherd wasn't going to bend. "Before the conference was over, we were both talking a little loud and I took the occasion to have the doors to my office closed," Craig recalled. "The outcome was that I did not get the additional ship, nor the missing rifle companies." Craig was soon justified in all his requests: "One month later ... we had to borrow and steal trucks from the Army to give us mobility." Despite the rather heated conference, Shepherd and Craig remained good friends.[16]

Upon his return to Washington, General Cates happened to run into the chief of naval operations (CNO), Admiral Forrest P. Sherman, in a Pentagon hallway. Cates quizzed him about why the Marines were not being considered for Korea. "What do you have?" asked the CNO. Cates replied that the Marines on the West Coast were ready to go. The CNO sent a cryptic message through the commander in chief of the U.S. Pacific Fleet to FMF-PAC asking, "How soon can you sail for combat employment in the Far East: (a) A reinforced battalion: (b) a reinforced regiment?" Colonel Victor Krulak, who had just reported aboard as the FMF-PAC operations officer, was approached by Colonel Gregon Williams, chief of staff. "We have to answer this." Krulak simply took the note, sat down at a nearby desk, and wrote, "(a) 48 hours. (b) Five days, including a Marine aircraft group," and handed the message back to Williams. "How do you know we can do that?" he asked in amazement. "I don't," Krulak said, "but if we can't, we're dead."[17] At the time, there was a move afoot to seriously downsize the Marine Corps.

Within days of their meeting, the president called up the reserves, bringing the 1st Marine Division up to strength. Thousands of men—reservists, 2nd Marine Division augmentees, regulars from posts and stations—poured into Camp Pendleton at all hours of the day and night. In a one-week period almost 14 thousand Marines arrived. Major General Oliver P. Smith took command of the division and Major General Field Harris took command of the air wing.

The magnitude of the task accomplished by the Marine Corps in the first ten weeks of the conflict may be judged from the fact that on 30 June 1950, the 1st Marine Division (Reinforced) at Camp Pendleton had an actual strength of six hundred forty-one (641) officers and seven thousand one hundred and forty-eight (7,148) enlisted and the 1st Marine Aircraft Wing at Marine Corps Air Station, El Toro, a strength of four hundred seventy-four (474) officers and three thousand two hundred two hundred fifty-nine (3,259) enlisted. On 2 August, 1950, the 1st Provisional Marine Brigade comprising some five thousand three hundred (5,300) ground officers and enlisted from the Division and 1,300 aviation officers and enlisted from the Wing was moving into combat in the hard pressed Pusan bridgehead in South Korea, and on 15 September, 1950, the 1st Marine Division (Reinforced), some 26,000 strong and the 1st Marine Aircraft Wing, of 3,800 men launched an amphibious assault at Inchon, Korea.[18]

Immediately after the brigade shipped out for Korea, Shepherd began working out the details of replacement drafts. The early commitment of the brigade and the heavy casualties it suffered cost it critical "foxhole" strength. Replacement Marines had to be shuttled piecemeal in planeload increments, and because of the shortage of aircraft, replacements were not arriving fast enough. Shepherd took a dim view of the delay. To help resolve this critical shortage he proposed a combination sea-air lift, which helped to alleviate the problem. On August 3, Shepherd directed the 1st Marine Division to send 10 officers and 290 enlisted replacements to the brigade. Two weeks later, he directed several Marine bases to send another three hundred men to Japan. Other drafts were organized to bring the 1st Marine Division and 1st Marine Aircraft Wing up to full war strength.[19] Additionally, Shepherd was directly involved in preparing the thousands of reserves pouring into Camp Pendleton for movement overseas, including seven trainloads of Marines from Camp Lejeune on January 10.[20]

CHAPTER 21

The Great Gamble, September 15, 1950

Inchon (Operation *Chromite*)

Inchon was the principal port of the west coast, Seoul the hub of the enemy's communication lines between North Korean invaders and North Korean troops pushing into the Republic of Korea. Capture of the two cities would simultaneously disrupt the North Korean People's Army's rear area and provide the UN forces with a valuable staging and supply point as well as air sites for further offensive operations. Capture of Wolmi-do, a fortified island in the Yellow Sea (connected by isthmus to the mainland), was necessary, or else the Navy convoy carrying Marines and soldiers would be subject to deadly bombardment.

On July 7, Shepherd flew to Tokyo for a conference with General MacArthur and the Joint Chiefs of Staff. "It was generally known that doubts and misgivings had been expressed at various times when the project was discussed at the Pentagon," General Joseph Collins, Army chief of staff, acknowledged. "Frankly, we were somewhat in the dark, and it was a matter of great concern, we went out to discuss it with General MacArthur."[1]

A considerable discussion took place on the feasibility of a landing at Inchon due to the exceptionally high rise and fall of the tide—some 30 feet—at the mouth of the Han River. At ebb tide mud flats extended from the shoreline to the channel. This prevented the beaching of landing craft except at the height of the flood tide, which occurred for only an hour or two twice daily. Furthermore, the most favorable high tide during September occurred on the 15th. Shepherd was flabbergasted when he learned that MacArthur had planned to make the landing on September 15. "It was already August ... and I couldn't imagine landing in Korea the 15th of September. I mean that was just a month away and we hadn't even formed the division."[2]

Finally, at Inchon the assault waves would land in the center of a fortified city with little maneuver flexibility in the populated area surrounding it.[3] "Inchon was a pretty damn tough spot to take. Initially I was lukewarm about making an amphibious landing in the center of a well-defended city. I was thinking about World War II, and the Japanese, and how they fought from house to house, and it was tough going. I was afraid we would run into similar difficulties at Inchon and it would cost the lives of many Marines to take the city."[4]

We Shall Crush Them

The Joint Chiefs proposed landing at some other beaches south of Inchon, but General MacArthur would not be swayed from his decision. He viewed the Inchon operation as the opening move in a strategic bid to crush the North Korean People's Army (NKPA). The seizure of the seaport city, only 25 miles from Seoul, would enable him to move rapidly against the capital and cut the NKPA's lines of communication and supply. Seoul was also the hub of an excellent railroad system and a road network that fanned north and south. Kimpo, the nation's best airport, lies between the two cities. Inchon was the key to the kingdom. No other port was satisfactory. Douglas MacArthur wanted the place, and being who he was, nothing was going to keep it from him—not the hydrographic conditions, not opposition, and certainly not the NKPA. MacArthur famously said, "We shall land at Inchon and we shall crush them!" After attending MacArthur's brief on Inchon, Chief of Naval Operations Admiral Forrest P. Sherman told Shepherd that he wished he had MacArthur's optimism.

General Wright, the operations officer of the Far Eastern Command, recommended that Shepherd be assigned to the command of X Corps. The Corps was composed of the 1st Marine Division and several Army divisions that had been formed to make the landing at Inchon, code-named *Chromite*. Shepherd brought the subject up in a conversation with

MacArthur, who responded that he would like to give Shepherd the command because of his distinguished combat record, but he had already promised it to his chief of staff. He did request that Shepherd accompany him on the operation as his personal amphibious adviser and said that he would have a full say in every decision. Shepherd was disappointed not to have been given command of the X Corps since he had contributed materially in making the landing possible. However, he couldn't criticize MacArthur for giving the command to his chief of staff, who was his closest military subordinate. Shepherd accepted MacArthur's offer to be his amphibious adviser, since the principal elements of the landing force were from the Fleet Marine Force, Pacific.[5]

The selection of Major General Ned Almond to lead the Corps was criticized because he lacked any experience in amphibious operations and did not recognize the difficulties inherent in the Inchon operation. Additionally, Almond and O. P. Smith did not get along. They were two different personalities. Smith was a cautious individual, a fine staff officer who carefully considered every contingency before taking action. Almond, on the other hand, was aggressive and anxious for X Corps to push ahead faster than Smith wanted. He also had an abrasive personality. According to his own second-in-command, Almond "could precipitate a crisis on a desert island with nobody else around."[6]

Shepherd tried to mediate between Almond and Smith. "I talked to O. P. and told him to play the game. Don't get so mad with Almond, he's trying to do the right thing." Almond didn't help matters. The first time he met Smith, Almond addressed him as "son." There was only a year age difference separating the two.[7]

Almond had several nicknames, according to Roy E. Appleman in *Escaping the Trap: The U.S. Army X Corps in Northeast Korea*.[8] "Generally, he was known to his friends and close associates as Ned. Other names were 'Ned the Anointed,' which meant he was a favorite of General MacArthur's, and 'Ned, the Dread,' which referred to his power, his brusque manner, and sometimes arbitrary actions."

Shepherd accompanied MacArthur to Sasebo harbor by automobile rather than plane to meet the USS *Mount McKinley*, the amphibious task force command ship, because of an approaching typhoon.

I rode on the back seat beside MacArthur. Just before sundown the clouds lifted and in the western sky a beautiful rainbow appeared. As we gazed at this lovely sight, General MacArthur turned to me and said, "Lem, there is my lucky rainbow. This operation is going to be a success. You know I commanded the Rainbow Division in France during World War I and I have always believed a rainbow is my lucky omen." Although General MacArthur placed great confidence in his own decisions, I always believed the rainbow that appeared in the sky at that psychological moment must have reassured him that the Inchon landing would be a successful operation.[9]

The *Mount McKinley* entered Sasebo harbor about midnight, but the strong wind and sea prevented the ship from tying up at the pier. Shepherd recalled, "It was necessary for members of our party to make a flying leap from the dock to a gangway, which had been lowered a few feet off the pier while still underway. The voyage through the Yellow Sea to Inchon was uneventful."[10] [11]

Friday, September 15, 1950, D-day

"The Navy and Marines have never shone more brightly"

GENERAL DOUGLAS MACARTHUR

"At daylight on the morning of September 15th the combat ships of the Naval Attack Force began their bombardment of Inchon and the adjoining beaches where the Marines were to land. Call to quarters was sounded at 0230, but I did not get up until 0530," Shepherd recalled. "It was a beautiful morning, and as the first pink streaks of dawn broke in the east my thoughts went back to other dawns when I had watched preparations for similar landings."[12] The *Mount McKinley* was at anchor some 13 thousand yards south of Wolmi-do, which belched fire as naval gunfire pounded the island. "I have never seen any better shooting. The entire island was smothered with bursting shells from the cruisers and destroyers, rockets from the LSMs, and napalm from the planes."[13] MacArthur watched from the admiral's bridge, as Shepherd observed. "His staff was grouped around him. He was seated in the Admiral's chair with his old Bataan Cap with its tarnished gold braid and a leather jacket on. Photographers were busily engaged in taking pictures of the General

Lieutenant General Shepherd and General MacArthur on flag bridge watching the assault on Wolmi-do. (U.S. Government)

while he continued to watch the naval gunfire—paying no attention to his admirers."[14]

Wolmi-do

Smoke obscured a portion of the denuded island—two days of napalm strikes had burned off the vegetation. The flagship hoisted the pennant, "Land the landing force," the order that sent wave after wave of LCVPs surging toward the enemy beach. Shepherd peered through his binoculars and watched the troops disembark and their movement to the line of departure. It was overcast, and smoke from the burning city made it difficult to observe the final run to the beach. As H hour approached,

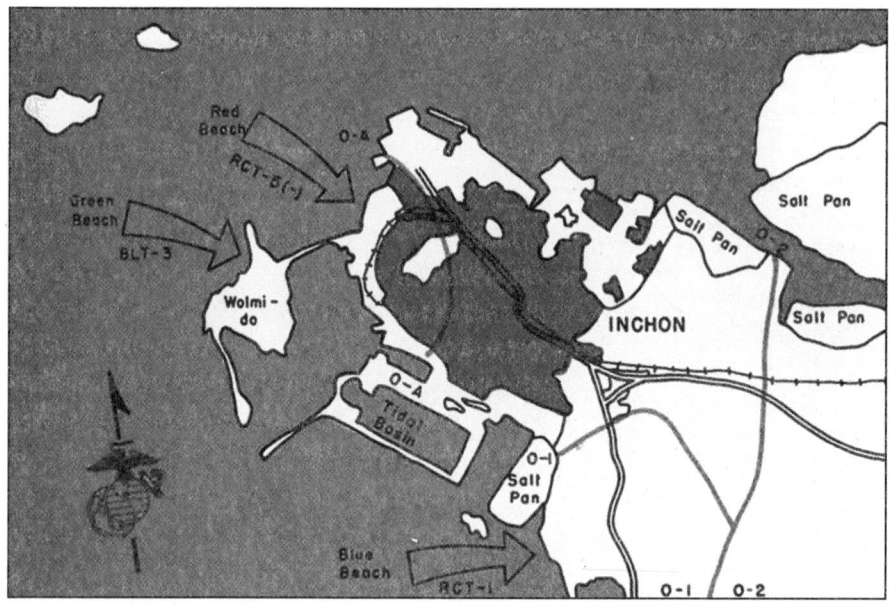

Schematic of the Inchon landing. (USMC)

the crescendo of fire increased. Promptly at 8:00 a.m. the 3d Battalion, 5th Marines landed on Wolmi-do, a small island opposite Inchon that was connected to the city by a causeway. An armored car was spotted. It was immediately knocked out by an air strike. North Korean resistance was relatively light, and within an hour the island was secured at a cost of four killed and 20 wounded. After the initial landing, sometime in midmorning, MacArthur insisted on going for a better look. The admiral's barge was called away.

Shepherd, Vice Admiral Arthur D. Struble, commander of Joint Task Force-7, and a few

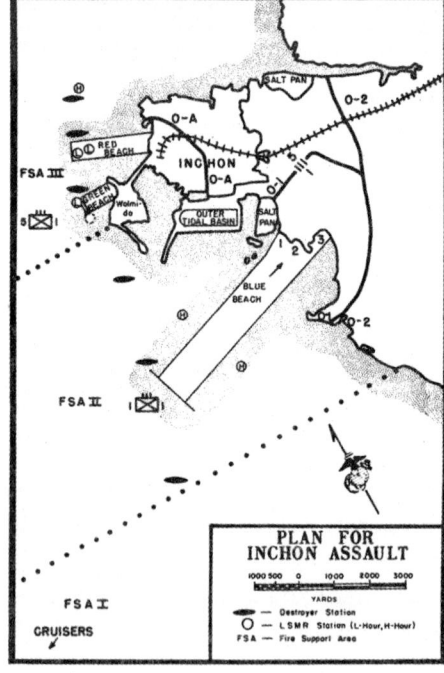

Plan for the Inchon assault. (USMC)

staff officers hitched a ride with MacArthur. Shepherd vividly recalled the drama.

> We all got in a boat together which took us to Wolmi-Do Island and then to the dock at Inchon to look that over. We then went around to another place [Red Beach] where there was a hell of a lot of fighting going on. Shells were falling all around the boat. I said, "For God's sake, general. It's dangerous to get too close to the shore." He didn't pay any attention and went right ahead. So, I said to Struble, "I don't think it's safe to take General MacArthur, the commander in chief of the theatre, in here and expose him to this rifle and mortar fire."

The boat turned aside and escaped. MacArthur's luck held. The North Koreans were not aware of the lucrative target. Struble caused hard feelings when he inferred that Shepherd was scared of getting into the beach. Shepherd fumed, "Well, I wasn't scared; it wasn't bothering me, but I felt a certain amount of responsibility for protecting General MacArthur from having a mortar shell hit the boat. So, I never had a damn bit of use for Struble after that."[15]

Later, Struble, Almond, and Shepherd set off again. As the admiral's coxswain lay alongside the Blue Beach seawall, a disheveled, dirt-encrusted Marine yelled out, "Lay off, you stupid bastards! We're going to blast a hole in the wall!" The coxswain replied, "This is Admiral Struble's barge." "I don't give a shit whose barge it is," said the Marine. "Get it clear before I blow the seawall!" "As we pulled out to sea," Shepherd recalled, "we could hear machine-gun and mortar fire all around the shoreline. The various fires were burning fiercely, and occasionally some oil storage tanks would go off and flames would leap way up in the air. It was a terrific sight and one I shall long remember."[16]

In the late afternoon flood tide, the main landing took place on the beaches south of the city, with the first wave touching the seawall at approximately 5:30 p.m. Along part of this area there was a stone breakwater that required the use of ladders to mount. Only light resistance was encountered, and the leading waves soon established a beachhead ashore. Upon receiving an official message from the landing force commander that the beachhead had been secured, MacArthur sent out a dispatch: "The Navy and Marines never shone more brightly."[17] Shepherd was a very proud witness. "I was right there when MacArthur took his pen and wrote it." After dictating the message, MacArthur turned to the group and said, "That's it, let's get a cup of coffee."[18]

In later years, Shepherd talked about the part he played in the Inchon operation: "I didn't realize it then, but I know now that, in my entire military career, it was the single most significant thing I did for my country."[19] During an interview, Shepherd stated, "MacArthur was, in my opinion, the greatest military leader in our country."[20]

That afternoon, MacArthur, Shepherd, and several staff officers took a sightseeing trip around the harbor, often close to the shoreline. "As the Coxswain came

Lieutenant Baldomero López leading his men under fire over the seawall at Inchon. He posthumously received the Medal of Honor for smothering a hand grenade with his body several minutes later. (USMC)

close to the shore line," Shepherd related, "I felt that MacArthur was being unnecessarily exposed to fire from the North Korean shore batteries. Apparently they were unaware of the lucrative target which was within close range of their guns as we were not fired on."[21]

Just before dusk, Shepherd accompanied one of the reserve battalions ashore. "Flames from the burning city lighted the sky along the entire waterfront. It was one of the most spectacular sights I have ever witnessed." Mortar shells forced Shepherd to return to the *Mount McKinley*, where he reported the operation's success to MacArthur. The following morning, the 1st Marine Division completed the capture of Inchon and was continuing the advance toward Seoul. General MacArthur wanted to go ashore and visit the troops. Shepherd and Almond accompanied him in a jeep along with several other jeeps filled with high-ranking officers, newspaper correspondents, and photographers on the Inchon–Seoul road. As the jeeps rounded a bend in the road, they came upon six smoldering

A Soviet-made North Korean T-34 tank knocked out during the United Nations advance from Inchon to Seoul after the amphibious landings at Inchon during the Korean War, circa mid-to-late September 1950. (NARA NA 80-G-421166)

T-34 North Korean tanks. Several dead North Korean soldiers lay around them on the road. A Marine captain stepped in front of the jeep and held up his hand, stopping them. Shepherd described the scene: "There were six tanks lined up on both sides of the road and burning with dead bodies lying half-cooked on top of several of the tanks.... The turrets had been punctured by clean hits."[22]

The captain told Shepherd that the six knocked-out tanks had been leading a North Korean counterattack that his company had just stopped by bazooka fire. The tanks and three hundred infantry from the 18th North Korean Division counterattacked Dog Company, 5th Marines. When the shooting stopped, all six tanks were destroyed and more than two hundred North Koreans had been killed. Shepherd said it was a dramatic moment and that MacArthur was "truly impressed and the Marines in the advance guard were also thrilled to see the General." General Almond, not so much. "You damn Marines always seem to be in the right place at the right time. You could not have staged a more spectacular performance if you had planned and rehearsed it."[23]

What Shepherd did not know was that seven fully armed North Koreans were flushed out of a culvert—the culvert where MacArthur's jeep had been parked—shortly after MacArthur's party left.[24]

Shepherd said the incident with the tanks was an example of MacArthur's courage and leadership in combat.

Whenever General MacArthur went ashore, as he did every day during the Inchon landing, he would always go forward as close as his jeep could carry him to the front—too close in my opinion for a Commanding General to be, as we were occasionally exposed to enemy fire. On several occasions when I was with him I would say, "General, don't you think we have gone far enough? I know you wish to talk to your front line troops but I am sure they worry about your safety when you expose yourself unnecessarily." He would talk to the unit commander about the enemy situation and in certain instances where an act of individual bravery was brought to his attention, General MacArthur would decorate the individual on the spot. In my opinion General MacArthur was truly a great military leader.[25]

On September 17, the 5th Marines secured Kimpo airfield, 21 miles south of Seoul. At 10 o'clock the next morning Shepherd and Krulak flew into Kimpo on an HO3S helicopter to become the first American aircraft to land there. The flight marked the culmination of Shepherd's long held belief that vertical flight would have significant impact on the Corps.

X Corps continued to advance against moderate resistance toward the Han River bridges, which, unbeknownst to the Marines, had been destroyed. The 1st Marines, under Colonel Lewis B. "Chesty" Puller, reached Yeongdeungpo, a large industrial suburb of Seoul. The town was well defended, and it took several days of hard fighting before it was captured.

The Liberation of Seoul

During the night of September 20, the 5th Marines erected a floating bridge across the Han River several miles west of Seoul and established a bridgehead on the opposite bank. By daylight the 5th and the 7th launched a coordinated attack from the northwest while the 1st Marines attacked from the south. The following day the 7th U.S. Army Division crossed the Han and joined in the attack. Shepherd gained a vantage point on the morning of September 20 to observe the crossing, which he thought was well executed without the loss of a single man.[26]

After the division crossed the Han River, there was increasing pressure to capture Seoul. MacArthur asked Shepherd every morning, "Lem, when are your Marines going to capture Seoul?"[27]

The liberation of Seoul dwarfed, by far, any previous single Marine combat objective. The city was a sprawling metropolitan area with a population of more than two million people, including thousands of terrified refugees. The city proper consisted of solidly constructed multi-floored office buildings that often fronted wide boulevards. The broad avenues offered excellent fields of fire for the defenders, who threw up barricades every four hundred to six hundred yards. They piled dirt- and rubble-filled rice bags eight feet high and six feet deep, reinforced with trolley cars, automobiles, and streetcar rails—anything to act as a barrier. They sowed mines around each barricade and covered them with machine guns and anti-tank weapons. The improvised strongpoints, stretching across the entire street, were centered on intersections for maximum effectiveness.[28]

The makeshift barricades were almost impervious to machine gun and small arms fire. Their destruction took a coordinated effort by infantry, tanks, engineers, and supporting arms. Even successful attacks often left a trail of killed and wounded Marines. Rifle companies in both regiments melted away. In the close-quarter door-to-door fighting, it was shoot first, ask questions later. The civilian population was caught in the crossfire; Seoul became a killing ground. It would not be captured without great difficulty.

As the days passed it became increasingly difficult for Shepherd to answer MacArthur's question ["Lem, when are your Marines going to capture Seoul?"] "I was in personal contact with General Smith and visited his command post daily. I knew the 1st Marine Division was making a determined effort to seize the city but were meeting determined resistance by its North Korean defenders, which I explained to MacArthur." General Almond wanted Seoul wrapped up—and he wanted it by September 25. At one point he inferred that the 1st Marine Division might not be up to the task and the 7th Infantry Division might be sent in to help the Marines. O. P. Smith took great exception to Almond's threat.[29]

Shepherd finally decided to answer MacArthur's question by simply replying, "We will capture Seoul today, general, which seemed to satisfy him." Fortunately, at about midnight on September 28, Shepherd received a personal dispatch from O. P. Smith: "Marines of the 1st Marine Division have captured Seoul." Shepherd was so elated by the news that he jumped out of bed in his pajamas and ran to MacArthur's cabin. "The general was pacing up and down, smoking his corncob pipe. Without apologizing for his informal attire, he said, 'General, we have captured Seoul. We've got it. I told you we would take Seoul today.'"[30]

Liberation Ceremony, National Palace

At 10:00 a.m. on September 29, MacArthur's plane, named SCAP (acronym for Supreme Commander Allied Powers), landed at Kimpo airfield. An impeccably dressed MacArthur and his wife stepped out onto the runway and climbed into the lead sedan. Other lesser dignitaries found room in one of the other four sedans or scrambled for space in one of 40 jeeps that comprised the convoy. Elaborate preparations had been made to ensure not only the safety of the celebrants but also the proper decorum of the proceedings. Concern about decorum may have been the reason why the Marines were not invited to the festivities.[31]

"The Marines were not represented in the ceremonies at the National Palace except General Smith, myself, Colonel Puller, my aide and one or two other officers," Shepherd recalled. "You'd think that they'd have the decency to give some of the honor to the men who captured the place." The five Marines wore combat gear and one, Puller, had a hard time even getting in. An Army MP, complete with white gloves and white bootlaces, barred his battered jeep from entering a "sedan only" entrance. Puller resolved the dilemma in short order by ordering his driver to "run [the MP] over."[32]

The National Palace still smelled of smoke and charred wood. The observers could clearly hear the sounds of distant small arms fire and artillery explosions. The interior was ringed with "a detachment of army military police wearing knife-pressed, tailor-made ODs [olive drab] with gleaming black airborne boots laced with white nylon parachute cords." Their snazzy appearance was in sharp contrast to the "out of sight" grungy Marines who were really providing security. Craig said, rather tongue in cheek, "The MPs looked more or less out of place at the time." O. P. Smith commented dryly, "The Marines were a little caustic about it."[33]

Craig's aide reported that the palace had glass ceiling panels that were weakened after all the shelling. Shards of glass were constantly fluttering down onto the concrete floor, making a tinkling noise as they hit. He watched as MacArthur escorted Syngman Rhee to a small podium in front of one hundred or so senior officer guests. MacArthur recited the Lord's Prayer and, after a short speech, turned to Rhee, saying, "Mr. President, I return your country to you."[34]

Wonsan (Operation *Yo-Yo*)

With the liberation of Seoul and the restoration of the South Korean government, the only mission remaining was the destruction of the North Korean People's Army. The battered remnant of that army was desperately attempting to escape north across the 38th parallel. Shepherd recalled that "General MacArthur conceived the idea of sending the 1st Marine Division around the east coast of Korea and make a landing at Wonsan, a port city on the east coast of North Korea. After the landing the Division was to make contact with the VIII Army. Then envelopment the North Korean Army, as he had done at Inchon."[35]

The 1st Marine Division boarded Japanese LSTs (gifts after World War II because the United States didn't need them) in Inchon Harbor and sailed around to the east coast, where the invasion fleet steamed back and forth for five days while the Navy cleared the harbor and sea approaches of an estimated two thousand mines. In the interim, South Korean troops captured Wonsan after a hard-fought battle. To add insult to injury, Bob Hope waited for the Marines on the beach, much to their chagrin.

CHAPTER 22

Attack of General Winter, November 1950

As the initial "Korean Conflict" developed into a first-class war, a major confrontation between nations, Shepherd established a forward command post in Tokyo, which he visited monthly. In November 1950, Shepherd visited the 1st Marine Division, which was advancing up the narrow winding road toward the Chosin Reservoir. The winter months were fast approaching bringing with it freezing weather and heavy snow. Shepherd believed that nothing could be colder than a winter in North Korea. Every effort was being made by my supply depots in Japan and South Korea to provide overcoats and heavy clothing.[1]

"Before we went up the mountain on our Marine Corps birthday, November 10, it was quiet enough for me to go swimming in the nearby stream—even though the water was a trifle cold for a guy from Atlanta," Lieutenant Colonel Raymond G. Davis, CO 1/7 recalled. "Ten days later the temperature dropped below zero. On our second or third day up on the plateau at Koto-ri, the Siberian winds struck, lowering the temperatures suddenly to sixteen degrees below zero … the arctic-like weather struck so suddenly that it sent men into shock, and they had to be led zombie-like, to shelter."[2]

Equipment died, particularly the battery-operated radios. Vehicles would not start. The drivers soon learned to run them all night long. A little too much oil or grease on a weapon caused malfunctions; carbines, machine guns, and BARs (Browning automatic rifles) were particularly susceptible. Artillery recoil mechanisms froze, and the cannoneers had to push the tubes back in battery by hand.

North to the Yalu, A New Enemy, Chinese Volunteers

The VIII Army continued to pursue the North Korean People's Army until it reached the 38th parallel, the boundary between North and South Korea. It was stopped at the border awaiting approval to cross into North Korea. MacArthur had great difficulty in getting permission from the president and the Joint Chiefs of Staff because of the threat the Chinese would intervene. The delay afforded the North Korean Army an opportunity to reorganize their forces.[3]

On September 27, the Joint Chiefs of Staff, in the name of the president, gave the go-ahead to cross the border, with the proviso that "at the time of such operations there has been no entry into North Korea by major Soviet or Chinese Communist forces, no announcement of intended entry, nor a threat to counter our operations in North Korea."[4]

Four days later, MacArthur authorized the release of a broadcast calling for the surrender of the North Korea People's Army, who did not dignify it with a reply. Two days later, however, the Chinese forwarded their intentions through a third-party intermediary. China's foreign minister, Zhou Enlai, confirmed via India's ambassador that if UN forces crossed the 38th parallel, China would provide support to the NKPA. Chairman Mao Zedong, leader of Chinese Communist party, had been carefully monitoring the American landings at Inchon and Wonsan and had ordered upwards of 260 thousand to 300 thousand Chinese "volunteers" into North Korea as early as October 13–14.

MacArthur's intelligence chief, Major General Charles Willoughby, failed to detect the presence of the Chinese troops, thus MacArthur told the president at their October 15 meeting on Wake Island that the war would be over by Thanksgiving and that even if China intervened, at most not more than 50 thousand troops would cross the Yalu. In fact, by October 19, 260 thousand Chinese Communist Forces (CCF) soldiers had already crossed into South Korea.[5]

The first patrols from the 1st Cavalry Division crossed the 38th parallel on October 7. Two days later the rest of the division followed and started fighting its way north. The Allied drive was going so well that there was almost an end to the war atmosphere. The *Stars and Stripes*, an Army–Air Force newspaper, quoted MacArthur as saying: "This war is definitely coming to an end shortly." Signs appeared throughout the area saying, "Drive carefully—the Marine you hit might be your relief."[6]

The 7th Marines received orders to relieve a Republic of Korea unit in contact with enemy troops on the road leading to the Chosin Reservoir. There were rumors that the enemy were Chinese "volunteers." The regimental commander told his men, "We can expect to meet Chinese Communist troops, and it is important that we win this first battle."[7] "The 7th Marines intelligence section reported that the CCF Fourth Field Army was crossing the Yalu into North Korea with the mission of preventing the X Corps from crossing into either China or Manchuria."[8]

"The first prisoners—Chinese prisoners—captured by the 7th Marines were within eighteen miles of Hŭngnam, and it was definitely a Chinese division, the 124th," Brigadier General Edward A. Craig, the assistant division commander, stated. "There was no doubt in the minds of the Marines that there was an organized group of Chinese troops in our front. If higher headquarters did not realize there was a Chinese buildup in this area, I do not know why."

During his visit on October 31, Shepherd was shown a group of Chinese prisoners. Upon his return to Tokyo, he had a long talk with General MacArthur about the identity of the prisoners and seemed quite concerned about them. Shepherd believed that MacArthur realized the danger, but he took the chance on their not entering the war.[9]

X Corps Withdrawal

O. P. Smith sent report after report to the Corps commander (Almond) about the massive Chinese force the division was up against.

> Every four hours we sent in a report of what was going on, but apparently they [X Corps] were stunned; they just couldn't make up their minds that the Chinese had attacked in force. They just had to re-orient their thinking. General MacArthur issued the order for withdrawal of the X Corps to Hŭngnam and their subsequent evacuation from North Korea.[10]
>
> Shepherd flew into Koto-ri for a firsthand appraisal of the withdrawal. He talked with General Smith about the plan for withdrawal and his desire to walk out with the troops. "I had known O. P. since the end of the First World War, and I thought he would welcome me as someone who could take some of the responsibility off his shoulders. Well, I was wrong. O. P. didn't like the idea at all.

"'General,' he said, 'please don't march down with us. No one wants to see a lieutenant general of Marines killed or captured.'" A chastened Shepherd reconsidered and decided to honor Smith's request. As he was about to board the evacuation aircraft, a very angry Marguerite Higgins, a well-known reporter for the *New York Herald Tribune*, showed up under escort by Colonel Lewis B. "Chesty" Puller. She wanted to walk out but Smith nixed the idea, which did not sit well with her. "This is the biggest story of the war," she pleaded. "I don't want to miss it, general." Shepherd, an old friend, tried to calm her down, with little effect. Later she wrote a scathing article claiming O. P. was prejudiced—but the story was squelched.[11]

Before the plane could take off, fighter-bombers had to work over the surrounding hills to knock out Chinese machine gunners. Shepherd and Higgins were crammed together in the cockpit of the overloaded aircraft. As it flew over the Communist gunners, Shepherd playfully remarked to Higgins, "Won't it be scandalous of we crash in each other's arms?" Marguerite's crass rejoinder would have done credit to a Marine gunnery sergeant.[12]

On December 4, Shepherd was assigned as Vice Admiral Turner Joy's personal representative at Hŭngnam to supervise the evacuation of X Corps.

The Hŭngnam Redeployment

Shepherd colocated his command post at General Almond's headquarters and worked closely with him in supervising the loadout operations. The division completed the loadout on December 14, and General Smith opened his command post aboard the USS *Bayfield*.

Shepherd believed that the withdrawal of the 1st Marine Division from the Chosin Reservoir Plateau to Hŭngnam was one of the epochal operations in the annals of the Marine Corps. The chill, misty dawn of Christmas Day found the USS *Mount McKinley* with Generals Almond and Shepherd after an eminently successful operation. The final statistics were staggering—105,000 military personnel, 91,000 Korean refugees, 17,500 vehicles, and 350,000 measurement tons of cargo loaded out in 193 shiploads by 109 ships.

Shepherd released a statement for the press upon his arrival back in Hawaii, in which he dismissed their accounts that the Marines were trapped and had to retreat.

> The opposing Chinese forces were so punished by the Marines as to constitute no further threat.... I believe that by no stretch of the imagination can this be described as a retreat, since a retreat presupposes a defeat—and the only defeat in this battle was the one suffered by the Chinese. Furthermore, when the Marines arrived in Hamhung, they had their arms, equipment, vehicles, and supplies with them. Their spirits were high and they were proud of their accomplishments.[13]

East-Central Front

The second year of the war found Shepherd's FMF-PAC supporting the 1st Marine Division and 1st Marine Aircraft Wing in a protracted land battle against Communist China's People's Volunteer Army and the North Korean People's Army. On February 20, 1951, the 1st Marine Division launched Operation *Killer* as part of a United Nations counteroffensive. The acting division commander, Brigadier General Lewis B. "Chesty" Puller, was dissatisfied with the amount of close air support (CAS) his division was receiving. Shepherd took up the issue with the commander of the Fifth Air Force and was able to work out a satisfactory solution. Unfortunately, the agreement did not last and the issue of CAS continued to be a sticking point for the Marines all the way through the Vietnam War, when the "single manager" concept was introduced. The concept involved assigning responsibility for managing all fighter, bomber, and reconnaissance aircraft to one individual. The Marines felt that this system delayed CAS response times or resulted in support not showing up at all.

MacArthur

During a stopover in Tokyo, Shepherd called on General MacArthur at FMF-PAC headquarters. During the course of their conversation, Shepherd detected a feeling of discouragement about the war. "The success of the Inchon Landing and capture of Seoul had raised MacArthur's hope of a speedy conclusion of the Korean conflict," Shepherd recalled. "The withdrawal from Northern Korea had dimmed those hopes and the ensuing stalemate of Allied Forces along a line south of the 38th parallel, I believe, was the cause for his apparent discouragement. I also believe General MacArthur felt that he was not getting enough military support required to win the war."[14]

In April 1951, MacArthur was relieved as supreme allied commander in the Far East and returned to Washington for retirement. He stopped off in Hawaii to place a wreath of flowers in the National Memorial Cemetery of the Pacific in Honolulu honoring the soldiers, Marines, and airmen buried there. Shepherd accompanied him and heard his brief remarks. At the conclusion, MacArthur said, "I know not the humbleness of their birth, but I can testify to the glory of their death."[15]

CHAPTER 23

20th Commandant of the Marine Corps, January 1952–January 1956

After completing a two-year tour as commanding general, Fleet Marine Force, Pacific, Shepherd was appointed as the 20th commandant of the Marine Corps on January 1, 1952, by President Harry S. Truman. "General Cates's four years as Commandant were drawing to a close and he did not choose to be reappointed. He went to the President and reminded him of his promise to select Shepherd after Cates, and that's what he did."[1]

Commandant of the Marine Corps flag. (USMC)

Time magazine published a short editorial after President Truman nominated Shepherd to succeed Cates as the commandant.

> National Affairs: TOP MAN OF THE MARINES
> *Time*, November 19, 1951
>
> Nominated by President Truman to be Commandant of the U.S. Marine Corps: Lieut. General Lemuel Cornick Shepherd Jr.
> Born: February 10, 1896, in Norfolk, Va., only son (two sisters) of Lemuel C. Shepherd, a physician. His mother was Emma Lucretia Cartwright of Nantucket.
> Education: Public schools in Norfolk; Virginia Military Institute.
> Family: Married Dec. 30, 1922 to Virginia Tunstall Driver, a strikingly handsome woman. Three children: two sons, Lemuel III, 26, and Wilson, 23,

both Marine lieutenants, and both married this year to naval officers' daughters. One daughter, Virginia, 22, also married this year, to a Marine captain her father's aide.

Appearance: Brawny (5 ft. 9 in., about 160lbs.), hard-eyed, balding, a trim, athletic, professional soldier.

Tastes: Rolls his own cigarettes, likes bourbon (two drinks), underwater spear fishing, fox-hunting and polo.

Early Career: Made up his mind to be a soldier when he was in short pants. Graduated from V.M.I, a 2nd lieutenant in 1917, led a platoon, then a company of the 5th Marines at Belleau Wood and St. Mihiel, came out with three wounds and a reputation for tenacity and courage (D.S.C., Navy Cross, two Silver Stars, Croix de Guerre). Returned from occupation duty in 1919 marked out for command, put in the standard series of tours prescribed for rising young officers: aide to the commandant, to President Harding, sea duty, foreign duty (China and Haiti), staff schools, C.O. of the President's guard at Warm Springs, Ga.

World War II: Was a hard combat leader in the South Pacific. As a colonel training the 9th Regiment, he kept up a relentless pace (often 18 hours a day); his insistence on perfection earned him the nickname, "Combat Ready." Every new marine got a talk from the C.O. Subjects: duty, self-discipline, religion (he is a devout Episcopalian). Became a brigadier general in 1943, then led the Cape Gloucester operation at New Britain. On Guam, his 1st Provisional Marine Brigade led one of the beachhead assaults; on Okinawa, Major General Shepherd led his 6th Marine Division to its objective early, wheeled, and lent a much-needed hand in the bitter street fighting for Naha, the capital city. In World War II he picked up two D.S.M.s, two Legions of Merit and a fourth Purple Heart. Postwar: Spent four years as C.O., first at the Amphibious Training School at Little Creek, Va., then at the Marine Corps Schools at Quantico, Va. In 1947 was called to Washington, in line for the job of Commandant with his friend, Clifton Gates. Gates, also the possessor of a topflight record, got the four stars on seniority. Shepherd, said the President, would have another crack at it. Shepherd became boss of the Fleet Marine Force in the Pacific in June 1950. Old-line Marine officers consider him a "schools" man, versatile, able, grimly serious, obsessed with combat training. "Life under General Shepherd," said a Marine officer last week, "is going to be very uncomplicated. All he's going to stress is combat readiness—today, tomorrow, next year, and four years from now."

Shepherd inherited a Corps of about 230,000 men and women, with more than 33,000 of them (1st Marine Division and 1st Marine Corps Aircraft Wing) actively engaged in combat that had already cost the Marine Corps 17,400 casualties; casualties were continuing to occur at the rate of 2,000 per month.

On January 2, one day after becoming commandant, Shepherd announced his plan to reorganize the headquarters. At 10 o'clock, he made an address to the headquarters staff setting the tone of his administration. "I have studied the matter carefully over a number of years and it is my conviction that improvement can be achieved through greater decentralization and by reducing the number of subordinates reporting directly to me. I intend to accomplish this by instituting a simple general staff organization of departmental character."[2]

He created a new office, chief of staff and assistant commandant, who would be assisted by a deputy chief of staff and a secretary of the General Staff. Plans and Policies Division would become the classic general staff divisions: G-1 (Personnel), G-2 (Intelligence), G-3 (Operations and Training), and G-4 (Logistics). The departments—Personnel, Inspector, Quartermaster General, along with agencies for Reserve Affairs, Public Information, Policy Analysis, Fiscal Affairs, and Administration—would function as special staff agencies under the chief of staff. The Division of Aviation would be elevated to the position of assistant commandant for air with a third star.[3]

"Now that I have actually assumed the duties of the Commandant of the Marine Corps, my attention is fixed squarely upon the heavy responsibilities that will rest on my shoulders for the next four years." In the succeeding six pages he outlined in detail his plan for reorganization.

The largest problem facing the Marine Corps was gaining statutory recognition as a separate air-ground service. This was partially but not completely achieved in the National Security Act of 1947. The act recognized that the Marine Corps included "fleet Marine forces of combined arms, together with supporting air components," but failed to give the Corps a seat on the Joint Chiefs of Staff (JCS) and left it vulnerable in other respects.

Then, in 1952, Congress passed Public Law 416, known as the "Marine Corps Bill," which granted the commandant a seat on the JCS in matters relating to the Corps and provided that the Corps be organized to include not less than three combat divisions and three aircraft wings. Department of Defense officials, the JCS, and President Truman all opposed the bill. Interestingly enough, the principal opposition spokesman was the chief of naval operations (CNO), Admiral Forrest Sherman, who insisted that the CNO commanded the Marine Corps.

Shepherd had to walk a fine line because Sherman was not in favor of the Marine Corps becoming a separate entity in the Navy, and he fought this tooth and nail. As commandant, he could not become too involved officially and be loyal to his superiors. He knew what was going on unofficially, but he could not direct the activities of those working for separation of the Marine Corps from the naval establishment.[4]

In Shepherd's first year as commandant, Public Law 416 was passed by Congress in June 1952 authorizing the Commandant to be a member of the Joint Chiefs of Staff (JCS) on matters concerning the Marine Corps. Before attending his first meeting, Shepherd went to see General Omar Bradley and informed him that he intended to carry out the provisions of the new law. Bradley told him that he opposed his presence himself but that, in accordance with the law, he welcomed Shepherd to the Joint Chiefs of Staff. Shepherd noted that, subsequently, he and Bradley became good personal friends.

Public Law 416 also established that "the Marine Corps shall be organized at not less than three combat divisions and three airwings, and such other land combat, aviation, and other services as may be organic therein, and except in time of war or national emergency declared by Congress the personnel strength of the Regular Marine Corps shall be maintained at not more than four hundred thousand." Later, in 1978, Public Law 95-485 made the commandant a "full member" of the JCS.

A year later, Sherman brought matters to a head when he attempted to exercise control over the Marine Corps. Shepherd attempted to settle the matter but without success: "I got nowhere, Sherman would not move." Shepherd brought the matter to the secretary of the Navy, who supported Shepherd's view.[5]

Shepherd believed that the broader the Marine Corps involvement in the nation's military affairs, the greater its overall usefulness would be. One of those efforts was the Security Guard Program, which was initiated in 1948, by agreement with the Department of State. Shepherd increased the standards for selecting Marines for duty to the extent that, by 1954, there were 682 carefully selected officers and men in the program, serving in detachments of five to 53, in 70 locations around the world.

One of Shepherd's lasting legacies was the growth and permanence of the Fleet Marine Force supporting establishment at Camp Pendleton, Camp Lejeune, Twentynine Palms, and the two supply bases at Barstow, California, and Albany, Georgia.

By all accounts, Shepherd's tenure as commandant was highly successful.

CHAPTER 24

Retirement, January 1, 1956

Inter-American Defense Board

In 1957, while Shepherd was serving on the JCS, the position of chairman of the Inter-American Defense Board came up. It was normally a two-year appointment that was passed around to the different services. It was the Navy's turn to take the chairmanship, and Admiral Burke, the chief of naval operations, was asked by Shepherd if the Navy wanted the assignment. He showed no interest, so Shepherd told him, "I'd like to be considered as your appointee for the job when it comes up." South America had always intrigued him. Two months after retiring as commandant, Shepherd was nominated and made chairman of the Inter-American Defense Board. He assumed the duty on February 1, 1957.

The board was formed during World War II with the idea of unifying the Latin American countries against attack by the Germans or the Communists, who were beginning to become active. There was a general plan for the overall defense of America. The board tried to standardize equipment, tactics, and techniques of the services and to promote friendly relations between the countries of the hemisphere.

Shepherd found the assignment interesting and important. The mission of the board was to form a general defense plan for all countries of South and Central America. All 21 countries of the Organization of American States had representation on the board. Shepherd breathed new life into the organization by increasing the number of meetings and acquiring additional officers. When his two-year term was up, he was reappointed

General Lemuel C. Shepherd Jr. stands with a group of cadets, circa 1980. (Virginia Military Institute)

for an additional term. Under Shepherd's leadership and diplomacy, the Inter-American Defense Board made substantial contributions towards the defense of the continent and promoted solidarity among the military forces of the republics of the Western Hemisphere.

General Lemuel C. Shepherd retired on October 1, 1959, after 42 years and six months of service. He moved to Warrenton, Virginia, the heart of Virginia hunt country. After a bad fall from a horse, he moved to La Jolla, California, in 1967, where he soon became a familiar figure at the nearby Recruit Depot, San Diego. The author noted during a visit to the Recruit Depot in the 1980s that the premier parking space by the depot headquarters continued to be marked with his name and four stars to ensure it was available at any time. For many years he returned East at least annually, usually in the fall, to visit VMI and Washington. He ordinarily would stay at the Army-Navy Club, where

Shepherd's headstone Arlington National Cemetery. (Courtesy of Bill Heneage)

a painting of him still resides. General Shepherd's wife passed away in 1989, and he died on August 6, 1990. Both are buried in Arlington National Cemetery.

A horse-drawn caisson bearing Shepherd's casket made its slow progress through Arlington National Cemetery to the burial site. A battalion of Marines in formal uniform served as escorts. General Shepherd is interred near the grave of General of the Army George C. Marshall, like Shepherd a Virginia Military Institute graduate.

Appendix A
Military Background

1913–17	Virginia Military Institute
1917	Commissioned; Word War I France, 5th Marines, Château-Thierry, Belleau Wood, Saint-Mihiel, Meuse-Argonne, Army of Occupation in Germany, Mapping World War I battlefields
1920–22	Aide to CMC, General Lejeune
1927–29	3d Brigade, China
1930–34	Garde d'Haiti
1934–36	XO, Marine Barracks, Washington, D.C., and director, Marine Corps Institute; Naval War College
1937–39	CP, 2nd Battalion, 5th Marines
1939–42	Director, Correspondence School, chief, F-3 Section, and commandant, Marine Corps Schools
1942–43	World War II, CO, 9th Marines, 3d Marine Division
1943–44	ADC, 1st Marine Division, Cape Gloucester operation
1944, CG	1st Provisional Marine Brigade, Guam operation
1944–46	CG, 6th Marine Division, Okinawa operation, Occupation of Tsingtao
1946	CG Troop Training Unit, Amphibious Training Command, Atlantic Fleet, postwar amphibious planning
1948–50	Assistant to commandant, Marine Corps Schools, postwar professional education, development of vertical envelopment concept, helicopters
1950–51	CG, FMF-PAC, Marine operations in Korea, Inchon landing, General MacArthur and the Marine Corps
1952–56	Commandant of the Marine Corps, role of CMC in Joint Chiefs of Staff deliberations; retirement
1956–59	Chairman, Inter-American Defense Board

Appendix B

Military Decorations

The Navy Cross

Distinguished Service Cross

Distinguished Service Medal with two Gold Stars and the Legion of Merit with Oak Leaf Cluster

Silver Star with two Oak Leaf Clusters, France 1918 and Korea 1950

Oak Leaf Cluster in lieu of a second Legion of Merit, China 1945

Bronze Star, China 1945

Purple Heart with two Oak Leaf Clusters, France 1918 and one Gold Star, Okinawa

Presidential Unit Citation with three Bronze Stars, Okinawa and Korea

Navy Unit Commendation with one Bronze Star, Guam and Cape Gloucester

Victory Medal World War I with four Bronze Stars, Aisne-Marne, St. Mihiel, Meuse-Argonne, and Defensive Sector Clasp, France 1918

Expeditionary Medal with one Bronze Star, China 1927–28, Haiti 1930

Yangtze Service Medal, Shanghai, China, 1927

American Defense Service Medal

American Campaign Medal

Asiatic-Pacific Campaign Medal with four Bronze Stars

China Service Medal, 1945

Victory Medal World War II

Navy Occupation Service Medal, 1945

National Defense Service Medal

Korean Service Medal with two Bronze Stars

United Nations Service Medal

French Croix de Guerre with Gilt Star, France 1918

French Fourragere, France 1918

Medaille pour la Bravoure Militaire (Montenegrin) with crossed swords and palm

Haitian Order of Honor and Merit

Haitian Distinguished Service Medal

Order of the Cloud and Banner, Second Grade, China

Republic of Korea Order of Military Merit Taiguk Medal with Gold Star

Korean Presidential Unit Citation

Bronze Plaque with Diploma Commemorative Especial, Brazil 1922–23

Naval Order of Merit, Grand Officer Argentine 1955

Naval Order of Merit, Grand Officer Brazil 1955

Grand Cross of Naval Merit of Spain 1955

Abdon Calderon, First Class, Republic of Ecuador 1956

Military Order of the Ayacucho, Grand Officer, Peru 1956

Grand Cross, National Order of Merit of Paraguay 1956

Military Medal of the Army, First Class Chile, 1956

Medal of Military Merit of Mexico, First Class of 1956

Legion of Honor, Grade of Commander, France 1957

Brazilian Order of Military Merit, Degree of Grand Officer, 1959

Commander of the Order of Couronne, Belgium, 1959

National Order of Military Merit of Paraguay, Grade of Grand Officer, 1959

Endnotes

Chapter 1

1. General Lemuel C. Shepherd, USMC (Retired), Oral history transcript (Oral History Collection, Marine Corps Archives Branch, History Division, Interviewed by Benis M. Frank and Col. Robert D. Heinl, 1966 and 1967,) 113. Hereafter: Shepherd, Marine Corps oral history.
2. General Lemuel C. Shepherd, "Memoirs, boyhood–1920," Virginia Military Institute Archives, Digital Collection of Lemuel C. Shepherd Papers, 8.
3. Shepherd, Marine Corps oral history, 114.
4. General Lemuel C. Shepherd, USMC (Retired), Oral history interview transcripts, 1966–1967, Korea War Oral History (Lemuel C. Shepherd Papers, Virginia Military Institute Archives, 1966–67). Hereafter: Shepherd, Korean War oral history, 10.
5. Ibid., 11.
6. Ibid., 12.
7. Ibid., 14.
8. Ibid., 15.
9. Shepherd, Marine Corps oral history, 116.
10. Ibid., 118.
11. Ibid., 119.
12. Ibid., 122.

Chapter 2

1. Col. Frederick Wise, *A Marine Tells It to You* (J. H. Sears and Co., 1929), 41.
2. Ibid.
3. Tom FitzPatrick, *Tidewater Warrior, The World War I Years: General Lemuel C. Shepherd, Jr., USMC, Twentieth Commandant* (Signature Book Printing, 2010), 121.
4. Shepherd, Marine Corps oral history, 120.
5. Ibid., 121.
6. Richard D. Camp Jr., *Leatherneck Legends: Conversations with the Marine Corps' Old Breed* (Zenith Press, 2006), 17.
7. Camp, *Leatherneck Legends*, 17.

Chapter 3

1. Camp, *Leatherneck Legends*, 18.
2. Ibid.
3. Ibid.
4. Ibid., 19.

Chapter 4

1. Shepherd, Marine Corps oral history, 126.
2. Ibid., 127.
3. Camp, *Leatherneck Legends*, 20.
4. Shepherd, Marine Corps oral history, 127.
5. FitzPatrick, *Tidewater Warrior*, 130.
6. Shepherd, Marine Corps oral history, 128.
7. FitzPatrick, *Tidewater Warrior*, 134.
8. Ibid., 141.
9. Shepherd, VMI oral history, 44.
10. Camp, *Leatherneck Legends*, 23.
11. FitzPatrick, *Tidewater Warrior*, 153.
12. Ibid., 150.

Chapter 5

1. Shepherd, VMI oral history, 48.
2. FitzPatrick, *Tidewater Warrior*, 183.
3. Ibid.
4. Ibid., 184.
5. Ibid.
6. Camp, *Leatherneck Legends*, 25.
7. Camp, *Leatherneck Legends*, 26.
8. Ibid., 27.
9. Ibid., 26.

Chapter 6

1. Camp, *Leatherneck Legends*, 26.
2. Ibid.
3. Ibid., 27.

4. Ibid.
5. Ibid., 30.
6. Shepherd, Marine Corps oral history, 128.
7. Ibid., 130.

Chapter 7

1. Shepherd, Marine Corps oral history, 132.
2. Ibid., 130.
3. Ibid.
4. Camp, *Leatherneck Legends*, 36.
5. Shepherd, Marine Corps oral history, 134.
6. Ibid.
7. Camp, *Leatherneck Legends*, 39.
8. Ibid., 40.

Chapter 8

1. Shepherd, Marine Corps oral history, 137.
2. Ibid.
3. Camp, *Leatherneck Legends*, 41.
4. Shepherd, Marine Corps oral history, 138.

Chapter 9

1. *History of the Second Battalion, Fifth Marines* (First Brigade, Fleet Marine Force, Marine Barracks, 1938), 13.
2. Shepherd, Marine Corps oral history, 139.
3. Ibid.
4. *History of the Second Battalion, Fifth Marines*, 13.
5. Shepherd, Marine Corps oral history, 140.
6. Allan R. Millett and Jack Shulimson, eds., *Commandants of the Marine Corps* (Naval Institute Press, 2004), 330.
7. Shepherd, Marine Corps oral history, 140.
8. Ibid.
9. FitzPatrick, *Tidewater Warrior*, 425.
10. Ronald J. Brown, *A Few Good Men: A History of the Fighting Fifth Marines* (Presidio Press, 2003), 9.

Chapter 10

1. FitzPatrick, *Tidewater Warrior*, 446–47.
2. Ibid., 448.
3. Ibid., 450.

Chapter 11

1. Alan Shapley, oral history interview (Oral History Collection, Marine Corps Archives), 32.
2. Ibid., 10.
3. FitzPatrick, *Tidewater Warrior*, 461.
4. Ibid., 464.
5. Ibid., 465.
6. Shepherd, Marine Corps oral history, 15.
7. FitzPatrick, *Tidewater Warrior*, 467.
8. Ibid., 474.

Chapter 12

1. FitzPatrick, *Tidewater Warrior*, 475.
2. Edwin H. Simmons, "Remembering General Shepherd," *Fortitudine, Bulletin of the Marine Corps Historical Program* XX, no. 2 (1990): 3.
3. Ibid., 5.
4. Ibid.
5. Ibid., 5–6.
6. James H. McCrocklin, *Garde d'Haiti: Twenty Years of Organization and Training by the United States Marine Corps* (United States Naval Institute, 1956), 207.
7. Simmons, "Remembering General Shepherd," 3.
8. Ibid., 6.

Chapter 13

1. Simmons, "Remembering General Shepherd," 6.
2. Camp, *Leatherneck Legends*, 111.
3. Ibid.
4. Ibid.
5. Ibid., 112.
6. Ibid., 112.

Chapter 14

1. Robert Debs Heinl Jr., *Soldiers of the Sea: The United States Marine Corps, 1775–1962* (Nautical & Aviation Publishing Company of America, 1991), 392.
2. Ibid., 394.
3. S. E. Smith, ed., *The United States Marine Corps in World War II: The One-Volume History from Wake to Tsingtao* (Random House, 1969), 481.
4. Frank O. Hough and John A. Crown, *The Campaign on New Britain* (Historical Branch, Headquarters U.S. Marine Corps, 1952), 95.
5. Ibid., 98.

Chapter 15

1. Camp, *Leatherneck Legends*, 123.
2. Ibid.
3. Ibid.
4. Camp, *Leatherneck Legends*, 119.
5. Ibid., 124.
6. Heinl, *Soldiers of the Sea*, 438.
7. Ibid., 458.
8. Camp, *Leatherneck Legends*, 129.
9. Jeter A. Isely and Philip A. Crowl, *The U.S. Marines and Amphibious War: Its Theory and Its Practice in the Pacific* (Princeton University Press, 1951), 374.
10. Camp, *Leatherneck Legends*, 130.
11. Ibid., 136.
12. Camp, *Leatherneck Legends*, 137.
13. Camp, *Lieutenant General Edward A. Craig, Warrior Six: Combat Leader in World War II and Korea* (Casemate Publishers, 2023), 102.

Chapter 16

1. Camp, *Leatherneck Legends*, 176.
2. Maj. Chas. S. Nichols, Jr. USMC and Henry I. Shaw, Jr., *Okinawa: Victory in the Pacific*, (Historical Branch, G-3 Division, HQ, U.S. Marine Corps) 64.
3. Bevan Cass, ed., *History of the Sixth Marine Division*, (Infantry Journal Press, 1948) 47.
4. Camp, *Leatherneck Legends*, 189.
5. Shepherd, Marine Corps oral history, 40.
6. Ibid., 41.
7. Shepherd letter, comments on the Okinawa monograph.
8. Shepherd, Marine Corps oral history, 42.
9. Ibid.

10. Captain Rikihei Inoguchi, Commander Tadashi Nakajima and Roger Pineau, *The Divine Wind* (Annapolis, MD: United States Naval Institute, 1958) 147.
11. Col. Joseph H. Alexander, *The Final Campaign: Marines in the Victory on Okinawa* (History and Museums Division, U.S. Marine Corps, 1996), 50.
12. Shepherd, Marine Corps oral history, 54.
13. Shepherd, Old Dominion University Libraries Digital Collection, Lemuel C. Shepherd oral history, September 19, 1978, 12. Hereafter: ODU oral history.
14. Cass, *History of the Sixth Marine Division*, 175.
15. Oral history interview with General Lemuel C. Shepherd, September 19, 1978.

Chapter 17

1. Cass, *History of the Sixth Marine Division*, 209.
2. Benis M. Frank and Henry I. Shaw Jr., *Victory and Occupation: History of U.S. Marine Corps Operations in World War II, Volume 5* (Historical Branch, U.S. Marine Corps, 1968), 564.
3. Shepherd, Marine Corps oral history, 97.
4. Cass, *History of the Sixth Marine Division*, 209.

Chapter 18

1. Simmons, "Remembering General Shepherd," 8.

Chapter 19

1. Robert Debs Heinl Jr., *Soldiers of the Sea: The United States Marine Corps, 1775–1962* (Naval Institute Press, 1962), 515.
2. Shepherd, Marine Corps oral history, 172.
3. Heinl, *Soldiers of the Sea*, 1962, 517.
4. Ibid.
5. Ibid.
6. Ibid., 518.
7. Alan Rems, "A Propaganda Machine Like Stalin's," *Naval History Magazine* 33, no. 3 (June 2019).
8. Millett and Shulimson, *Commandants of the Marine Corps*, 318. Chapter 20: Fleet Marine Force, Pacific 99.

Chapter 20

1. Richard D. Camp Jr., *Three War Marine Hero: General Raymond G. Davis* (Casemate, 2023), 103.

2. Ibid.
3. Shepherd, Marine Corps oral history, 178.
4. Ibid., 178–79.
5. Henry Berry, *Hey, Mac, Where Ya Been? Living Memories of U.S. Marines in the Korean War* (St. Martin's Press, 1988), 35.
6. Camp, *Leatherneck Legends*, 200–201.
7. Ibid.
8. Lemuel C. Shepherd, Jr., Korean War Oral History, 1966, "The Interview with General Lemuel C. Shepherd, Jr." by Philip P. Brower, MacArthur Memorial, September 22, 1970," Virginia Military Institute, 4. Hereafter: Shepherd, Korean War oral history.
9. Camp, *Warrior Six*, 129.
10. Bower, The Interview, 6.
11. Ibid.
12. Heinl, *Victory at High Tide: The Inchon-Seoul Campaign* (J. B. Lippincott & Company, 1968), 19.
13. Lynn Montross and Captain Nicholas A. Canzona, *U.S. Marine Operations in Korea 1950–1953, Volume II: The Inchon-Seoul Operation* (Historical Branch, U.S. Marine Corps, 1955), 11.
14. Heinl, *Victory at High Tide*, 21.
15. Camp, *Leatherneck Legends*, 205.
16. Camp, *Warrior Six*, 137–38.
17. Robert T. Donald, US Army (Retired), "From Santo Domingo to Korea: The Biography of Major General Gregon A. Williams," unpublished manuscript.
18. "A Report on the activities of Fleet Marine Force Pacific from 25 June 1950 to the Amphibious Assault at Inchon" (Headquarters, Fleet Marine Force, Pacific, 1950), https://www.koreanwar2.org/kwp2/usmc/039/m039_cd14_1950_06_1120.pdf.
19. Ibid.
20. Montross and Canzona, *U.S. Marine Operations in Korea*, 31.

Chapter 21

1. Montross and Canzona, *U.S. Marine Operations in Korea*, 44–45.
2. Shepherd, Marine Corps oral history, 58.
3. Shepherd, Korean War oral history, 11.
4. Camp, *Leatherneck Legends*, 229.
5. Shepherd, Korean War oral history, 13.
6. Stanley Weintraub, *MacArthur's War: Korea and the Undoing of an American Hero* (The Free Press, 2000), 120.
7. Camp, *Warrior Six*, 171–72.
8. Roy E. Appleman, *Escaping the Trap: The U.S. Army X Corps in Northeast Korea, 1950* (Texas A&M University Press, 2000).

9. Shepherd, Korean War oral history, 14.
10. Ibid., 15.
11. Camp, *Leatherneck Legends*, 234.
12. Ibid.
13. Ibid.
14. Heinl, *Victory at High Tide*, 89, 93.
15. Camp, *Leatherneck Legends*, 238.
16. Ibid.
17. Shepherd, Korean War oral history, 16, 19.
18. Camp, *Leatherneck Legends*, 238.
19. Millett and Shulimson, *Commandants of the Marine Corps*, 338.
20. Camp, *Leatherneck Legends*, 168.
21. Shepherd, Korean War oral history, 17.
22. Ibid., 19.
23. Ibid., 19, 20.
24. Montross and Canzona, *U.S. Marine Operations in Korea*, 152.
25. Shepherd, Korean War oral history, 20.
26. Ibid.
27. Camp, *Leatherneck Legends*, 248.
28. Ibid., 246.
29. Ibid., 248, 249.
30. Ibid., 250, 251.
31. Ibid.
32. Ibid.
33. Ibid.
34. Ibid., 252.
35. Shepherd, Korean War oral history, 29.

Chapter 22

1. Shepherd, Korean War oral history, 32–33.
2. Camp, *Three War Marine Hero: General Raymond G. Davis*, (Philadelphia & Oxford: Casemate Publishers, 2020), 125.
3. Shepherd, Korean War oral history, 30.
4. Camp, *Warrior Six*, 190.
5. Ibid.
6. Ibid., 192.
7. Ibid., 193.
8. Camp, *Three War Marine Hero*, 129.
9. Shepherd, Korean War oral history, 30.
10. Ibid., 34.
11. Ibid.

12. Camp, *Leatherneck Legends*, 276.
13. Ibid., 279.
14. Shepherd, Korean War oral history, 40.
15. Ibid.

Chapter 23

1. Shepherd, Marine Corps oral history, 189.
2. Millett and Shulimson, *Commandants of the Marine Corps*, 340.
3. Ibid.
4. Shepherd, Marine Corps oral history, 174.
5. Millett and Shulimson, *Commandants of the Marine Corps*, 345–46.

Bibliography

Anderson, Col. William T. USMCR (Ret). *The Bravest Deeds of Men: A Fieldguide for the Battle of Belleau Wood*. History Division U.S. Marine Corps, 2018.

Alexander, Col. Joseph H. *The Final Campaign: Marines in the Victory on Okinawa*. History and Museums Division, U.S. Marine Corps, 1996.

Appleman, Roy E. *Escaping the Trap: The U.S. Army X Corps in Northeast Korea, 1950*. Texas A&M University Press, 2000.

Berry, Henry. *Hey, Mac, Where Ya Been? Living Memories of U.S. Marines in the Korean War*. St. Martin's Press, 1988.

Bower, Philip P. The Interview. Lemuel C. Shepherd Papers, Virginia Military Archives. September 22, 1970.

Brown, Ronald J. *A Few Good Men: A History of the Fighting Fifth Marines*. Presidio Press, 2003.

Camp, Richard D., Jr. *Leatherneck Legends: Conversations with the Marine Corps' Old Breed*. Zenith Press, 2006.

Camp, Col. Richard D. USMC (Ret.) *Three War Marine Hero: General Raymond G. Davis*. Casemate, 2023.

Camp, Col. Richard D., USMC (Ret.) *Lieutenant General Edward A. Craig. Warrior Six: Combat Leader in World War II and Korea*. Casemate Publishers, 2023.

Carlton, Phillips D. *The Conquest of Okinawa: An Account of the Sixth Marine Division*. Historical Division Headquarters, U.S. Marine Corps.

Cass, Bevan G., ed. *History of the Sixth Marine Division*. Infantry Journal Press, 1948.

FitzPatrick, Tom. *Tidewater Warrior, The World War I Years: General Lemuel C. Shepherd, Jr., USMC, Twentieth Commandant*. Signature Book Printing, 2010.

Frank, Benis M., and Henry I. Shaw Jr. *Victory and Occupation: History of U.S. Marine Corps Operations in World War II, Volume 5*. Historical Branch, U.S. Marine Corps, 1968.

Heinl, Robert D., Jr. *Soldiers of the Sea: The United States Marine Corps, 1775–1962*. Naval Institute Press, 1962.

Heinl, Robert D., Jr. *Victory at High Tide: The Inchon-Seoul Campaign*. J. B. Lippincott & Company, 1968.

History of the Second Battalion, Fifth Marines. First Brigade, Fleet Marine Force, Marine Barracks, 1938.

Hough, Frank O., and John A. Crown. *The Campaign on New Britain*. Historical Branch, Headquarters U.S. Marine Corps, 1952.

Inoguchi, Captain Rikihei, Commander Tadashi Nakajima and Roger Pineau. *The Divine Wind: Japan's Kamikaze Force in World War II*. Annapolis, MD: United States Naval Institute, 1958.

Isely, Jeter A., and Philip A. Crowl. *The U.S. Marines and Amphibious War: Its Theory and Its Practice in the Pacific*. Princeton University Press, 1951.

McCrocklin, James H. *Garde d'Haiti: Twenty Years of Organization and Training by the United States Marine Corps*. United States Naval Institute, 1956.

Millett, Allan R., and Jack Shulimson, eds. *Commandants of the Marine Corps*. Naval Institute Press, 2004.

Montross, Lynn, and Captain Nicholas A. Canzona. *U.S. Marine Operations in Korea 1950–1953, Volume II: The Inchon-Seoul Operation*. Historical Branch, U.S. Marine Corps, 1955.

Nichols, Major Chas. S. and Henry I. Shaw. *Okinawa: Victory in the Pacific*. Washington, D.C.: Historical Branch, G-3 HQ USMC. U.S. Government Printing Office, 1955.

Rems, Alan. "A Propaganda Machine Like Stalin's." *Naval History Magazine* 33, no. 3 (June 2019).

"A Report on the activities of Fleet Marine Force Pacific from 25 June 1950 to the Amphibious Assault at Inchon." Headquarters, Fleet Marine Force, Pacific, 1950. https://www.koreanwar2.org/kwp2/usmc/039/m039_cd14_1950_06_1120.pdf.

Shapley, Alan. Oral history interview. Oral History Collection, Marine Corps Archives.

Shepherd, General Lemuel C., USMC (Retired). Oral history transcript. Oral History Collection, Marine Corps University Archives.

Shepherd, General Lemuel C., USMC (Retired). Oral history interview transcripts, 1966–1967. Lemuel C. Shepherd Papers, Virginia Military Institute Archives, 1966–1967.

Simmons, Edwin H. "Remembering General Shepherd." *Fortitudine, Bulletin of the Marine Corps Historical Program* XX, no. 2 (1990).

Simmons, Edwin H., and Gordon W. Keiser. "The U.S. Marine Corps and Defense Unification, 1944-47: The Politics of Survival." *Naval War College Review* 38, no. 4 (1985). https://digital-commons.usnwc.edu/nwc-review/vol38/iss4/21.

Smith, S. E., ed. *The United States Marine Corps in World War II: The One-Volume History from Wake to Tsingtao*. Random House, 1969.

Vandegrift, A. A., and Robert B. Asprey. *Once a Marine: The Memoirs of General A. A. Vandegrift, USMC*. W. W. Norton and Company, 1964.

Weintraub, Stanley. *MacArthur's War: Korea and the Undoing of an American Hero*. The Free Press, 2000.

Wise, Col. Frederick. *A Marine Tells It to You*. J. H. Sears and Co., 1929.

Index

Page numbers in **bold** *refer to illustrations.*

aircraft, 50–51, **50**, 121
Almond, Major General Edward M.
  "Ned," 137–38, 145, 149, 153, 160
amphibious techniques/operations, 71–72,
  84, 85–87, 92–95, 108, 123, 128, 130
Appleman, Roy E., 145
artillery, 30–31, 38–39, 43, 49, 54, 55,
  85–86, 96, 109

Barnett, Major General George, 5, 13–14,
  59, 74
Barrett, Major Charles D., 58, 63–64
Belleau Wood, x, 37–41
  casualties, 49
  first Germans killed, 44–45
  German advance, 40, **41**, 43–44
  Hill 142, 38, 65
  Les Mares Farm, 39–40, 64, 65
  medals awarded to Shepherd, 44, 48,
    61, 66
  monument, 125–26, **126**
  outposts, 43–44
  relief map of, 63–66
  relieved of duty and attacked by
    Germans, 45–46
  scalding accident, 64
  Shepherd is wounded, 43–44, 46–47
Benson, Admiral W. S., 14, 59
billets, 20–21, 26
Blanchfield, Captain, 29, 39, 43, 45
Blanc Mont (White Mountain)
  casualties, 55–56
  German defenses, 53–54
  post-war mapping of, 65
  Shepherd is wounded, 56–57
  Shepherd's worst day of the war,
    October 4, 1918, 53–56
Boxer Rebellion, 9
Bradley, General Omar, 166
British Army, 69
Brown, Colonel Preston, 37
Bruce, Major General Andrew D., 85
Buckner, General Simon B., 92–93, **92**,
  103–4, **105**
Buford, Gunnery Sergeant David L., 44
Buse, Lieutenant Colonel Henry W., 80
Butler, Captain, 10, 29

camions (trucks), 34–35, 51
Cape Gloucester, 77–78
  Aogiri Ridge, 78, 79–80
  Hill 660, 80–81
  Suicide Creek, 79–81
casualties, 30, 49, 55–56, 79, 87, 97,
  98–99, 102, 106, 107
Cates, Major General Clifton B., 129–30,
  131, 135, 139, 140, 141, 163
Chancellorsville, battle of, 6
Château-Thierry, 37, 38
Chen Pao-Tsang, Lieutenant General,
  117, **119**
Chiang Kai-shek, 117
China, 68–69, 115–22
  Communist activity, 117, 121

Korean War, 158–60
local Japanese surrender, 116–17, **118**, **119**, **120**
mob action, 118
Tsingtao, 115–17, 121
Chō, Lieutenant General Isamu, 100
Civil War, 1, 6
Clement, Brigadier General William T., 113
Collins, General Joseph, 143
"The Commandant's Own" (drum and bugle corps), 71
Connelly, Rear Admiral R. L. "Close In," 86
conscription, 5
Coroveau, Lieutenant, 55–56
Courtney, Major J. L., 103
Craig, Brigadier General Edward A., 89–90, 137, 140–41, 159
Craige, Captain John, 67
Cumming, 1st Lieutenant Samuel Calvin, 32–33
Cushman, Brigadier General Thomas J., 136, 137

Davis, Lieutenant Colonel Raymond G., 157
defense unification 1944–1947, 127–31
    Edson Board, 128
    Key West Agreement, 130–31
    U.S. Marines fight for survival, 127–28
    Vandegrift's "Bended Knee Speech," 129
Dessez, Captain Paul T. "Bobo," 6
Doyen, Colonel Charles A., 5–6
Driver, Virginia Tunstall, 68
dugouts, 32

Eby, Kerr, *Ghost Trail*, **78**
Edson, General Merritt A., 128, 129
Eisenhower, Dwight D., 125

Feland, Colonel Logan, 53, 54, 68
Fessenden Fifes, 69
"First to Fight" slogan, 10, 13, **14**

Fleet Marine Force, Pacific, June 1950, 133–42
    Korean War, 133–42, **135**
    meeting with MacArthur, 137–40
    Operation Plan 2–50, 137
Forrestal, James V., 120
Fort Douaumont, 34
foxholes, 39
France Map Detachment, 63
French Army, 115th Battalion Chasseurs Alpins ("Blue Devils"), 21–25, **22**
French language, 21, 22–23
frontline duty, 30–32
    no-man's-land patrol, 32–33

Geiger, General Roy S., x, 99, 104, 105, 108, 109
George Washington, USS, 58, 59, 64–65
German Army, advance at Belleau Wood, 40, **41**, 43–44
Gibbons, Floyd, 35
Guadalcanal, 75–77, 83–90
Guam, 83–90

Haiti, 69–70
Halsey, Admiral William, 113
Hancock, USS, 11–12
Harris, Major General Field, 141
Henderson, USS, 12–13, **13**, 15–17
Higgins, Marguerite, 160
Hindenburg line, 53
Hodges, Colonel Harry, 5
horses, 1, 37, 67, 70, 131, 170
hospitals, 46–47, 56
Idaho, USS, 68
Inchon, 143–44, 146–47
inspections, 25, **135**
Inter-American Defense Board, 169–70
interwar years, 1920–1943
    aide-de-camp, 67
    command of 2d Battalion, 5th Marines, 71–72
    foreign service in China, 68–69
    Garde d'Haiti, 69–70

international exposition, 67–68
Marine Barracks, Washington, 70–71
Iwo Jima, 123–25, **124**

Jackson, Stonewall, 6
Japan
    capitulation, 112
    surrender of troops in China, 116–17, **118**, **119**, **120**
Japanese troops, 78, 79–81, 86, 88–89, 96
    banzai tactics, 97
    battle flag, **95**
    battle slogan, 95
    defenses, 99
    hari-kari, 110, 112
    suicide operations, 93
Johnson, Louis S., 130, 136
Joy, Vice Admiral Turner, 137
jungle warfare, 77–78, **78**

Kiki (Sheperd's dog), 27, 46, 47, 48
Korean War
    China's role, 158–60, 161
    close air support (CAS), 161
    D-Day, September 15, 1950, 146–47
    East-Central Front, 161
    Hŭngnam redeployment, 160–61
    Inchon, 143–44, 146–47, **148**, 149–50, **150**
    Liberation Ceremony, National Palace, Seoul, 154–55
    liberation of Seoul, 152–54
    north to the Yalu, 157–58
    police action, Korean War, 133–42
    Wolmi-do, 147–52, **147**
    Wonsan, 155
    X Corps withdrawal, 159–60
Krulak, Lieutenant Colonel Victor H., 92, 103, 105, 137, 140, 141, 152

Lejeune, Major General John A., 53, 59, 67

MacArthur, General Douglas, 81, 134, 137–40, 139

Korean War, 143–52, **147**, 153–55, 158, 161–62
    Shepherd's admiration for, 150, 151–52
Mao Zedong, 158
marches, 26–27, 45, 49
"Marine Brigade," 66
Marine Corps, 5–6, **11**
    assistant commandant and chief of staff, 123–26
    headquarters reorganization, 165
    new recruits, 10–11
    organization, 10
    probationary examination, 63
    reductions of, 127–28, 130–31, 136
    seal, 125, **125**
    Shepherd as 20th Commandant, 163–67, **163**
    uniforms, 125
    War Memorial, Washington, 123–25, **124**
Marine Corps Schools, Quantico, 73, 131, 133
Marine Corps units
    1st Marine Brigade, 83–90, 138–39
    1st Marine Division, 135, 137, 141–42, 150, 153–54, 155, 157, 160, 161
    3d Marine Division, 85, 89, 99–100
    4th Marine Brigade, 25, 39, 53, 59–60, 69
    4th Marine Regiment, 83–84, 85, 87, 88, 89, 96–99, 106, 108, 110, 112, 113
    5th Marine Regiment, 7–8, 9, 10, 14, **16**, **20**, 25, 29, 50, 54–55, 71–72
    6th Machine Gun Battalion, 25
    6th Marine Division, 91–113, 115–17, 121, 122
    6th Marine Regiment, 25, 50
    7th Marine Regiment, 77, 80, 80–81, 111, 159
    9th Marine Regiment (Striking Ninth), 73–76, **75**, 89

22nd Marine Regiment, 84, 85, 88, 100–101, 102, 107, 108, 111–12
29th Marine Regiment, 96–99, 105–6, 107, 108, 109, 110, 112
55th Company, 5th Regiment of Marines, 9, 10–11, 29, 31, 38, 45–46, 47–48, 49, 55–56, 57
83rd Company, 6th Marines, 67–68
Combat Team A, 77
Marine Aircraft Group 32 (MAG-32), 121
Marine Aircraft Group 33 (MAG-33), 136
Marshall, General George C., 127
Matthews, First Lieutenant Bill, 45
McDonough, Gordon L., 131
medical services, 46–47, 56
memorials, 123–26, **124**, **126**
Menacourt, 19, 20, 25
Motobu Peninsula, Battle of, 96–99, **97**
Mount McKinley, USS, 145–46, 150, 160
Mt. Vernon, USS, 74–75
mud, 31, 49

Nagano, Major General Eiji, 116–17, 119, **119**
Nash, Charlie, 7
National Security Act 1947, 129, 130, 165
Naval Appropriations Act, 5
naval bombardment, 86, 146–47
Neville, General Wendel, 58, 60
Newman, USS, 115
New York, victory parade, 59
New Zealand, 75
Nichols, General Edward W. "Old Nick," 5, 6
Noble, Colonel Alfred, 74–75
North Korean People's Army, 133–34, 140, 143, 144, 155, 158, 161

Officers School of Application, 7
Okinawa, x, 91–95
    landing plan, **94**
    U.S. flag raised, 112

Operation *Backhander*, 77
Operation *Chromite*, 143–44
Operation *Downfall*, 112
Operation *Iceberg*
    Ara Saki Peninsula, capture of, 111–12
    Asakawa River, crossing of, 100–101
    casualties, 97, 98–99, 102, 106, 107
    Motobu Peninsula, Battle of, 96–99, **97**
    Naha, capture of, 106–7, **107**
    Okinawa, assault and capture of, 91–95, **94**
    Oroku Peninsula, Battle for, 107–11
    Sugar Loaf Hill, 101–3, **102**, 105–6
Operation *Killer*, 161
Operation *Stevedore*
    beach landings, 85–87
    casualties, 87
    final drive, 89–90
    Operation Plan Number 1, 85
    Orote Peninsula, 87–89
Operation *Yo-Yo*, 155
Ord Jr., Colonel Retired James B., 69
Ōta, Rear Admiral Minoru, 107, **108**, 111, 112

Paris, 27–28, 37, 56–57
    Fourth of July parade, 47–48
Parris Island, South Carolina, 7
patrols, 31, 43, 76
    in no-man's-land, 32–33
Pearl Harbor, 72, 73, 83
Pershing, General John J., 25
Pétain, General Henri, 25
Philadelphia Navy Yard, 8, 9, **11**
Public Law 416, 165–66
Puller, Brigadier General Lewis B. "Chesty," 152, 154, 160, 161

Radford, Admiral Arthur W., 133, 134, 135, 137
reconnaissance, 31–32, 38, 95, 106, 109, 115, 116–17, 121
refugees, 37–38, 117–18
Rio de Janeiro, 68

Roberts, Colonel Harold, 111–12
Robinson, Captain Fielding, 56–57
Roosevelt, Franklin D., 59, 71
Rosenthal, Joe, 124
Russell, Major General John, 70–71

Saint-Mihiel, September 1918, 49–51
Schneider, Colonel Merlin F., 85
sea sickness, 16
Security Guard Program, 166–67
Selective Service Act, 5
Senate Bill 2044, 127, 128–29
Shapley, Lieutenant Colonel Alan, 83–84, 85, 109
Shepherd, Emma Cartwright, 1, 27, 59
Shepherd, John Camp, 1
Shepherd, Virginia Cartwright "Siddie," 69, 164
Shepherd, Wilson E. D. "DeeDee," 68, 163–64
Shepherd III, Lemuel C. "Bo," 68, 163–64
Shepherd Jr., Major General Lemuel C., **ix**, ix–x, **55**, **91**, 93, **119**
    20th Commandant of the Marine Corps, 163–67, **163**
    amphibious adviser to MacArthur, 145–46
    applies for a Marine appointment, 5–6
    arrival in France, **16**, 17
    assistant commandant and chief of staff, Marine Corps HQ, 123–26
    birth, 1
    career details, 163–64, 173
    childhood and education, 1–2
    children, 68, 69, 163–64
    commandant of Marine Corps schools, Quantico, 131, 133
    command of Fleet Marine Force, Pacific (FMF-PAC), 133–42, **135**
    death and burial, 171, **171**
    decides to remain in the Marine Corps after WWI, 60–61, 66
    embarks on USS *Henderson*, 12–13, 15–17
    engagement and marriage, 68
    fishing trip, 134–35
    graduates VMI, 6
    and horses, 67, 70, 131, 170
    leadership style, 74, 84
    letters home, 15, 24–25
    military decorations, 44, 48, 61, 81, 176–77
    in New York, August 1919, 59
    occupation duty in Germany, 57
    in Paris, 27–28
    pet dog, 27, 46, 47, 48
    placed in command of a platoon, 9, 10, 16
    promotion to Brigadier General, 76
    promotion to Captain, 57
    promotion to Colonel, 73
    promotion to Lieutenant Colonel, 71
    promotion to Major, 70
    promotion to Major General, 92
    reputation for tactical competence, 54
    retirement, 169–70, **170**
    as a student, 3
    victory parades, 59–60
    VMI Cadet, 2–6, **2**, **4**
    wounded in action, 43–44, 46–47, 56–57
Sherman, Admiral Forrest P., 141, 144, 165–66
Short, Walter, 72
Smith, General "Howlin' Mad," 83, 88, 89
Smith, Lieutenant General Holland M., 100, 104
Smith, Major General Oliver P., 141, 145, 153–55, 159–60
Smith, Major General Ralph C., 100, 104
Smithsonian Institution, 65
Sol Navis, USS, 63
Sprague, Vice Admiral Thomas, 137
standard operating procedures (SOP), 75
Stars and Stripes, 158–59
Stilwell, Lieutenant General Joseph W., 104–5

Struble, Vice Admiral Arthur D., 148–49
submarines, 5, 16–17
Sullivan, John, 129–30
supplies, 75

tanks, 72, 79, 84, 87, 88, 101, 150–51, **151**
    tank-infantry doctrine, 92
tent camps, 19, 68
Time magazine, 163–64
Toussaint, Major, 22
training, 7, 17, 74, 75, 84, 92, 121–22
    with the "Blue Devils," 21–25, **22**
    Bourmont-Damblain Training Area September 1917–May 1918, 25–27
    Gondrecourt Training Area, July to September 1917, 19–25
    infantry tactics and weapons, 23–25
train journeys, 19–20, **20**, 27, 29–30
trench systems, 23, **23**, 24, 30, 31, 49
    living conditions, 34
    trench routines, 32
Troop Training Unit (TTU) Atlantic, 123
Truman, Harry S., 129, 130, 131, 134, 163
Turnage, Major General Allen H., 85
Turner, Admiral Richmond Kelly, 84, 160
Twining, Colonel Merrill B., 128

Udo, Colonel Takehiko, 96, 97
United Nations Security Council, 134
U.S. Army
    2nd Battalion, 55, 57
    2nd Division, 26, 29, 37, 39, 50, 53, 57, 58, 59
    3rd Army Brigade, 53, 54
    23rd Infantry, 54
    27th Division, 100, 103
    77th Infantry Division, 85, 89
    Tenth Army, 92–93, 103–4

Ushijima, Lieutenant General Mitsuru, 93, 99, **99**, 112

Vandegrift, General Alexander, 129
Vandegrift, General Alexander A., 83, 123, 128
Verdun, 29–30, 34
Virginia Military Institute (VMI), 2–6
    life at VMI, 2–3
    Tiqua Club, 3
Voss, Lieutenant, 56
Walt, Lieutenant Colonel Lew "Silent Lew," 79–80
Washington, D.C., 59–60
    Marine Barracks, 70–71
weapons, 23
    37mm guns, 80
    Bangalore Torpedoes, 49
    machine guns, 43–44, 45, 65, 79
    minenwerfer shells, 45
    mortars, 79, 110
    training, 74, 75
weather conditions, 26, 49, 77, 100, 157
Weldon, Felix de, 123–26
Whaling, Colonel William J., 105
Williams, Brigadier General R. P., 69
Williams, Colonel Gregon, 135, 141
Willoughby, Major General Charles, 158
Wilson, Woodrow, 14, 60
Wise, Major (later Colonel) Frederic May "Fritz," 9–10, 11, 19, 23, 27, 34–35, 45
World War I, 3, 5
    armistice, 1918, 57
    United States declares war, 5
Wright, General, 144

Zhou Enlai, 158